Master Your Money
Or It Will Master You

Arlo E. Moehlenpah, D.Sc.

Master Your Money Or It Will Master You

Copyright © 1999
Arlo E. Moehlenpah

Published by:

www.DoingGood.org
E-mail: Moehlenpah@aol.com

Cover design by: Paul Povolni

Cataloging-in-Publication Data
Moehlenpah, Arlo E., 1936-
    Master your money or it will master you

    Includes bibliographical references and indexes

ISBN 0-9667054-1-6

    1. Finance, Personal. 2. Finance, Personal-Religious Aspects
-Christianity

    I. Title.

HG179.M64 1999   332'.024–dc21

Printed in the USA by Morris Publishing
3212 East Highway 30 • Kearney, NE 68847 • 1-800-650-7888

Acknowledgements

This book is the result of teaching a class in personal finance at Christian Life College in Stockton, California. I thank God for the opportunity to teach this class and for the students, who contributed in many ways, including asking thought provoking questions. Most of what I know I have learned from others. I have tried to carefully document the sources of my information. I apologize for any errors or omissions. I especially want to acknowledge the contributions of Bill Gothard, Malcolm MacGregor, Larry Burkett, and Ron Blue for their writing and seminars, which have had a great influence on my thinking.

In addition, I want to thank and specifically mention the following people for their contributions to this book. My wife, Jane, produced the camera-ready copy. My daughter Glenda, who is an accountant; my son Ed, who is a computer specialist; Brenda Leaman, who is a pastor's wife; and Bill Harden, who is a Personal Financial Advisor and Registered Representative, proofread the book and made valuable suggestions. Bill also wrote the foreword. Robert Rodriguez, a car salesman, made suggestions regarding Chapter 10 – Buying a Car, and Darrell Isaacs, who is a real estate broker, made many improvements to Chapter 11 - Renting or Buying a Home. Rich Brown, who is an English teacher, gave editing suggestions for the final copy.

I also want to thank God for the physical and mental strength He has given us to accomplish this project.

The images used throughout most of the book were obtained from IMSI's MasterClips Collection, 1895 Francisco Blvd. East, San Rafael, CA 94901-USA.The images used in Chapter 5 were obtained from the Microsoft Office 97 Clip Gallery 3.0 Clipart.

Preface

The Title Of The Book

The title for this book, *Master Your Money Or It Will Master You*, was selected after considerable thought. Jesus said that you cannot can serve two masters, referring to God and money (Matthew 6:24). Also, the writer of Proverbs, implies that the lender is master of the borrower (Proverbs 22:7). It is unfortunate to see so many people who have money as their master. This can take the form of being a "workaholic," trying to get ahead in this world at the expense of neglecting more important priorities, or of being in such bondage to debt that they are not even free to pray or do other aspects of God's will. Scripture gives much instruction regarding money as emphasized in Chapters 3 and 4.

My first attempt for a title was *What I Wish I Knew About Money When I Was Your Age*. This title, though, implied that I was only writing to people much younger than myself, when actually the book includes topics, such as planning for retirement and stewardship after death, which are applicable to people my age or older. Another title suggested was *What My Parents Forgot To Tell Me About Money*. The problem with this title was that it implies that I include nothing my parents taught me about money, when perhaps much of what I know I learned from them.

What The Book Is About

In addition to biblical principles, this book includes many interesting topics such as goal setting, developing a spending plan, getting out of debt and staying out of debt, money saving tips, buying a car and a home, investing, and stewardship. It also discusses the implications of a mother of young children working outside the home.

Format Of The Book

This book is written in a question and answer format. The reader may choose topics of greater interest at the time and obtain answers to his questions without having to read extensively.

Purpose Of The Book

There is an old saying, "an ounce of prevention is worth a pound of cure." It is true that experience is a good teacher, but it can be a hard and expensive way to learn. It is hoped that by reading this book, the readers can be spared many of the problems resulting from poor financial management. Even for those who are in the midst of these problems, it is never too late to start to learn. Hopefully, the information in this book will help them get through these problems and avoid future ones.

Intended Audience

I would like to get the principles of this book into the hearts and minds of all young people before they have to make a living on their own. Unfortunately, some who are having every need supplied by their parents will see this information about as relevant to them as resume writing skills to a kindergarten child. They will perhaps have to learn these lessons the hard and expensive way. The tendency toward divorces and other financial problems could be avoided by learning from the history of others who have encountered these problems.

Married couples will definitely see the value of this book because it deals with situations they are currently facing. Older people will especially benefit from the sections that cover retirement and provision for death. They also might want to give a copy to or teach some of the material to couples who are about to be married or are recently married.

This book also can be used as a text for a personal finance course in Christian schools and Bible colleges.

Foreword

As a personal financial advisor, I am often faced with the traumatic effects that follow in the wake of poor stewardship. Undisciplined lifestyles, which succumb to greed, ego, and self-indulgence, are easy prey for our buy-now—pay-later, credit card society. This mode of operation, which begins as an innocent necklace of desire, can easily become an evil noose of destruction.

Arlo Moehlenpah, in this book on the principles of financial management, addresses some biblical and practical principles, which are vital if one is to remain protected against the barrage of influences which war against responsible stewardship. He alerts the reader regarding the symptoms of Financial Problems so that the problems can be arrested before they become a disease.

Christians desiring to be effective in the Lord's work can certainly benefit from the advice in Chapter 7, "Getting Out of Debt and Staying Out." Using the author's insightful tips when purchasing an automobile or home could result in thousands of dollars saved and avoidance of hurtful "buyer's remorse."

Since believers follow a different standard than unbelievers, it should not be difficult for us to see the need to invest for the future to "provide for our own" (I Tim. 5:8). The legacy of the faithful steward can live on after death, if one will give astute attendance to the author's recommendations concerning Estate Planning.

This book is not only recommended reading but also a tremendous resource for the serious steward. What a valuable tool to pass on to young people, students and newlyweds! No doubt the application of this work will result in many hearing the words, "Well done, good and faithful servant."

Bill Harden
Personal Financial Advisor
Registered Representative

Table of Contents

Chapter 1 - The Need For Financial Planning

About 80% of our waking day is consumed in thinking about money: making it, saving it, spending it or giving it away.[1] If our money isn't managed well, everything else is out of balance.

What major problems can result from poor money management?

1. **Family problems.** Most individual tension, family friction, strife, anger, and frustration are caused, directly or indirectly, by money.[2] It has been estimated that 75% of all families suffer severely from stress and tension caused by unnecessary money problems. There is no end to the number of heartbreaking and relationship-breaking problems arising out of money matters. A professor of psychology at California State University claimed that 90% of all illness is caused by money worries, and that money worries are about 75% of all worries.[3]

   Money trouble is the number one cause of stress and failure in marriage and accounts for the majority of divorces.[4] A typical scenario is as follows: An average young couple, say Tom and Sally, try to accumulate in about three years what should take them thirty years to accumulate. They borrow to buy things they can't afford thus incurring a huge debt. Huge financial pressures come as a result of huge debt. The couple stops communicating and become combatants rather than companions. They find it hard to study the Bible and pray when their minds are consumed with problems. Sally unexpectedly gets pregnant and has to quit work. Tom loses his job. They separate, and, after losing their home and car, they still owe $16,000.[5] Can this be prevented? Yes. This is why there is such a need for financial planning.

2. **Inability to accomplish God's Will**. Many college students have had to drop out of school because they were not able to make their debt payments and school payments. The cares of this world and the deceitfulness of riches are some of the thorns that choke out fruitfulness (Matthew 13:22). "No one engaged in warfare entangles himself with the affairs of this life, that he may please him who enlisted him as a soldier" (II Timothy 2:4). A candidate who has major debts to pay cannot be approved for foreign missionary service, nor is a man free to start a home missionary church when he is entangled financially.

3. **Foreclosures.** When a person is severely behind in payments, a lending institution can foreclose and take possession of the item being purchased.

4. **Bankruptcy.** The number of people in the U.S.A. who filed for personal bankruptcy in 1996 exceeded one million for the first time ever. More than 90% were the result of out-of-control credit card debt. Credit card delinquencies are approaching 4%. The typical American carries an average balance of $1,900 per charge card, and some carry as many as eight to ten credit cards.

5. **Inability to retire.** Very few Americans are able to retire on the assets they have accumulated. Most either have to continue working or are dependent on charity, relatives, or the government to have enough money to live.[6]

6. **Suicide.** Severe financial pressure has caused people to have thoughts of committing suicide. Many people jumped out of windows to their death when the stock market crashed during

the depression of the 1930's.[7] Recently, it was noted that Las Vegas, Reno and Atlantic City, three of the nation's top cities with legalized gambling, have higher suicide rates than comparably sized cities without gambling.[8]

Can these problems be corrected? Yes, if people will follow biblical principles.

---

[1] Burkett Larry, *Your Finances in Changing Times*, World Wide, A ministry of the Billy Graham Association, 1303 Hennepin Avenue, Minneapolis, MN, 1977, 13.

[2] Ibid., 39.

[3] Galloway, Dale E., *There Is A Solution To Your Money Problems*, G/I, Regal Books, Glendale, CA, 16.

[4] Burkett, Larry, *The Complete Financial Guide For Young Couples*, Victor Books, Chariot Victor Publishing, a division of Cook Communication, Colorado Springs, CO, 1993, 11.

[5] Ibid., 11-13.

[6] Blue, Ron, *Master Your Money*, Thomas Nelson, Inc., Nashville, TN, Revised and updated edition, 1991, 13.

[7] Nelson, Sharon, "Money – A Wonderful Servant – A Terrible Master," unpublished article.

[8] The Record, "Study: Suicide rate higher in three major gambling cities," December 17, 1997.

Chapter 2 - Symptoms Of Financial Problems

In chapter one I mentioned some major problems that result from poor money management. In this chapter I will deal with some symptoms of these problems. To diagnose a physical problem, a doctor will often ask what symptoms you are having, such as a runny nose, a cough, headaches, sore throat or pain. To diagnose an automobile engine problem, a mechanic will ask for symptoms such as overheating, stalling, or excessive use of oil. On the basis of the symptoms, he will then attempt to treat the problem before it becomes too severe.

What are some symptoms of financial problems?[1,2,3,4]

1. Daily expenditures charged to credit cards due to lack of funds.

2. Current bills paid with savings or with advances on other credit cards.

3. Depreciating items purchased on credit.

4. Taxes and bills paid with borrowed money.

5. Overdue bills.

6. Deceitfulness. Purchasing on credit when you know you are behind on present obligations.

7. Greediness. Always wanting more. A burning desire to accumulate wealth and possessions can result in financial bondage.

8. A get-rich-quick attitude.

9. Covetousness. "Keeping up with the Joneses."

10. No gainful employment. Many who desire to start at the top never get started at all.

11. Family needs unmet. Luxuries may deprive family of needs, such as medical or dental care.

12. Self indulgence:

   A. purchasing without regard for usefulness

   B. lifestyle of lavishness

   C. consistently trading car

   D. closets full of clothes seldom or never used

   E. frivolous spending

   When you feel like you just have to go buy something to make you feel better, WATCH OUT. A person buying a car experiences a temporary high. So also does a person who purchases clothes, a motor home, a boat, or a stereo. If you feel like you need to have a spending spree, STOP AND GET COUNSEL - RIGHT NOW.

13. Over-commitment to work. So wrapped up in work that you have no time for your family.

14. Money entanglements.

15. An independent spirit. His money/her money attitude. "Separate but equal" will never work in a marriage. Withholding is one wedge Satan will use to split the marriage.

16. Lack of response to a fellow Christian who is in need.

17. Lack of communication. Failure to discuss short-range and long-range goals with your spouse or parents. What would you do if the breadwinner died suddenly?

18. Arguments with spouse or parents over finances.

19. Little white lies to your spouse or parents. When they learn the truth from another source they wonder what else is being kept secret.

20. Financial unfairness such as pressuring widows to make frivolous investments or pressuring young couples to buy unneeded insurance.

21. Unexplained fatigue. This could signal that your body is reacting to emotional stress.

22. Irresponsibility. Blaming someone or some circumstance for your debts.

23. The ostrich technique. Hiding your head in the sand. In other words, avoiding reality and pretending that no problem exists, and not responding to notices from creditors.

24. Religious escape. "I'm trusting God to provide." Creditors will not buy the "faith" idea.

25. Parent loans. If you are frequently requiring parents to bail you out, you are in trouble. If you get into trouble through overspending, get yourself out. BITE THE BULLET. When parents excessively help newlyweds financially they may encourage the young couple to be dependent on the parents or to live beyond their means. Wealthy parents of a wife can usurp the husband's authority, and the husband may resent it. This lowers self-esteem. Instead, adopt a pay-as-you-go basis. Financial trials can test our faith and commitment.

26. Wife working outside the home. When a wife has to work outside the home to provide basic needs, you may be living above your means. (See Chapter 12.) More money won't help because it's likely you'll "need" even more. More money is not the answer, more DISCIPLINE is.

27. Bill consolidation. This won't solve the problem of over-spending that must be corrected first. Self-discipline must be learned.

28. No tithe. Finding it difficult to give God His tenth.

29. Income = outgo. Or worse yet, when your income is less than your outgo, your spending becomes your downfall. Five percent of net spendable income should be set aside for non-allocated savings.

A principle I learned in chemical engineering is called a material balance.

Input

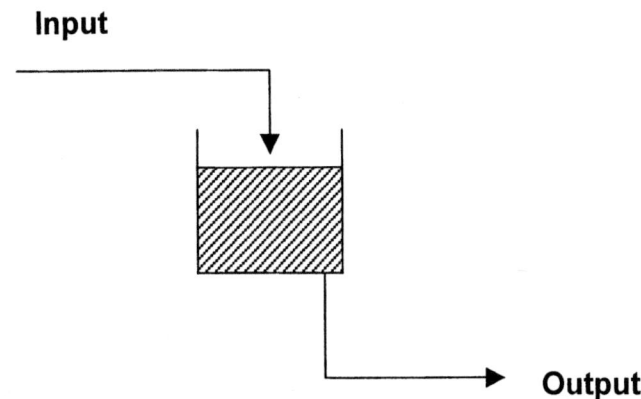

Output

Input minus Output = Change in Accumulation

Income minus Expenditures = Change in Savings

This principle applies not only to chemical engineering but also to dieting and finances.

30. No savings for emergencies.

31. No investments for the future.

32. Investment worries. Just worrying about money will not change anything.

33. Inadequate insurance. Emergencies do occur. Life insurance is needed in case the major income earner dies. Automobile insurance is needed in case of accidents. Medical insurance reduces the cost of hospitalization.

Always spend less than you make and remember it's better to earn interest than to pay it. Unfortunately, dealing with the symptoms might not correct the problems. However, recognizing the symptoms makes you aware that you have problems. The following chapters give advice that should help solve the problems.

---

[1] Burkett, *The Complete Financial Guide For Young Couples*, 40-47.

[2] Ibid., 93-104.

[3] Burkett, *Your Finances in Changing Times,* 59-65.

[4] Galloway, 80-84.

Chapter 3 - Make God Your Partner

What must a person recognize regarding God and finances?

1. God knows your needs (Matthew 6:32).

2. God wants to supply your need (Philippians 4:19). Jehovah-jireh means Jehovah will provide.

3. God even wants to give you the desires of your heart (Psalm 37:4).

   Who is your source of supply? Your employer? Your own cleverness? Another person? God? The first three will fail, but not God.

Why should you make God your source of supply?

1. God owns all the real estate - the earth is the Lord's (Psalm 24:1).

2. God owns all the cattle on a thousand hills (Psalm 50:10).

3. God owns the financial world. "The silver is Mine, and the gold is Mine" (Haggai 2:8).

   There are no shortages with God. He is able to do exceeding, abundantly, above all we ask or think (Ephesians 3:20). God has infinite avenues of supplying your need.

Why should a person tithe?

Before you can expect the harvest, you must first plant the seed. "A tithe is not a debt we owe but a seed we sow."[1] The first act of worship recorded in the Bible was the giving of an offering to the Lord by Cain and Abel (Genesis 4:3-4).[2] However, the first indication of the proportion of one's goods to be given was when Abram gave a tithe (tenth) of everything to Melchizedek (Genesis 14:20). When Jacob awoke from his dream of a ladder to heaven, he vowed he would give God a tenth of all that God gave him. Thus, tithing originated long before the Law of Moses. Under the Mosaic Law, God ordained tithing as a means of supporting the priests and the Levites. It is interesting to note that Hezekiah reinstated the bringing in of tithes as part of a revival of righteousness (II Chronicles 31:5-6). Centuries later, Nehemiah also restored the practice of tithing as an integral part of his "revival" (Nehemiah 10:37, 12:44). In the New Testament, Jesus talked to scribes and Pharisees who tithed of mint and anise and cummin but omitted the weightier matters of the Law. He said that they should have done both (Matthew 23:23). Paul also talked about the support of the ministry. He said a soldier expects support, an owner of the vineyard eats of the fruit, and a keeper of a flock drinks the milk. He also said that those who ministered in the temple got their food from the temple, and those who served at the altar shared in what was offered on the altar. In the same way, the Lord has commanded that those who preach the gospel should receive their living from the gospel (I Corinthians 9:6-14).[3] Thus, tithing was a biblical practice throughout the entire Bible. It is true that in the Book of Acts some gave all they possessed, but, as a bare minimum, I believe you should give a tenth (tithe) of what you earn. One person said everyone pays tithes, but some pay it to doctors, lawyers, etc. Why not give the tithe to God who can bless you? God said, "Prove me ... if I will not open you the windows of heaven and pour you out a blessing, that there shall not be room enough to receive it" (Malachi 3:10 KJV). I personally believe, with God as your partner, you will do far better with 90% than you would do alone with 100%. Blessings include health, food, clothing, shelter and transportation, to name a few.

Should a person pay tithes on "gross" or "net" income?

It is common practice today for items such as income taxes, Social Security, medical insurance and payroll savings to be deducted from your paycheck. We refer to our wages before anything is deducted as our "gross" income, and what remains after deductions as our "net" income. Until the last few decades, no employer provided this convenience for employees. If your rent, car payments and other bills were deducted also, would you only pay tithes on what remained? No, it would only mean that someone was kind enough to pay some of your bills out of what you earned. I don't think there is any question that you should pay tithes on your "gross." That is what you earn. Deductions are merely expenses that are being paid.[4] Social Security deductions are perhaps one exception. A person could give tithes on Social Security payments after retirement rather than on the deductions when they are withheld. This would give the senior citizen the feeling of still being involved in the support of the church. Also, a person would not need to give tithes on income tax returns if they had already given tithes on the gross.

God can multiply what we give to Him. If we sow sparingly, we will reap sparingly. If we sow bountifully, we will reap bountifully (II Corinthians 9:6). The widow of Zarephath gave all she had, a handful of meal and a little oil, and God multiplied it many times until another source of food was provided (I Kings 17:8-16). You can expect a return of unlimited supply. Solomon said, "One man gives freely, yet gains even more; another withholds unduly, but comes to poverty" (Proverbs 11:24 NIV). He also said, "Honor the LORD with your possessions, /And with the firstfruits of all your increase; /So your barns will be filled with plenty, /And your vats will overflow with new wine" (Proverbs 3:9-10). Putting God first is called firstfruits.

James said you don't have for two reasons. Either because you don't ask, or else because you ask for the wrong purpose (James 4:2-3). Jesus said, "Give, and it will be given to you: good measure, pressed down, shaken together, and running over will be put into your bosom. For with the same measure that you use, it will be measured back to you" (Luke 6:38).

Another way to make God your partner is to do things for other people. Jesus said with regard to giving food, drink, or clothing that "inasmuch as you did it to one of the least of these My brethren, you did it to Me" (Matthew 25:35-40). Solomon said, "He who has pity on the poor lends to the LORD, /And He will pay back what he has given" (Proverbs 19:17).

What are some purposes that God has for our finances?

1. To provide basic needs such as food, drink, and clothing (Matthew 6:31).

2. To illustrate God's power (Malachi 3:10-11).

3. To unite Christians (II Corinthians 8:14-15, Acts 11:27-30). God allows some financial situations to give Christians an opportunity to help other Christians.

4. To confirm direction (Philippians 4:19).

What are some reasons why there are times when God doesn't provide funds?

1. Perhaps you don't need what you are wanting.

2. Maybe God is testing your faith.

3. Maybe you have misspent your other funds, or perhaps you have violated scripture.

4. Maybe God wants a major change in your life (location, method, or vocation).

---

[1] Galloway, 114.

[2] Nelson, 4.

[3] Ibid., 4-12.

[4] Ibid., 14-15.

Chapter 4 - Money - An Important Biblical Subject

It is claimed that more is said in the New Testament about money than heaven or hell or almost any other topic. Some of the words that are used are abundance, contentment, coveting, giving, gold, mammon, pounds, silver, talents, treasures and wealth. Five times more is said about money than about prayer.[1] Also, many of Jesus' parables and illustrations deal with money. The Bible addresses virtually every financial decision a person will ever make.

What are some topics the Bible deals with regarding money?

1. **Stewardship.** God owns everything that we have.[2] An owner has rights; a steward has responsibilities. A steward is one who manages the resources of another person. Each of us is a manager, not an owner. A Christian who refuses to relinquish ownership can never experience God's plan for his finances.[3] We possess much but own nothing. Someday we will give an accounting. Resources involve money, time and talents. Stewardship is the use of God-given resources for the accomplishment of God-given goals. Your checkbook certainly reveals much about what you believe about stewardship.[4] For a man to be in spiritual leadership "He must be one who manages his own household well" (I Timothy 3:4 NIV).[5] Also as a steward of God, a bishop must be blameless (Titus 1:7).

2. **We are in the growth process.** Money is a test as well as a tool. "If you have not been faithful in the unrighteous

mammon, who will commit to your trust the true riches? And if you have not been faithful in what is another man's, who will give what is your own?" (Luke 16:11-12).[6] Sometimes financial problems are a test. To have your faith perfected it must be tested (James 1:2-4).

3. **The amount is not important.** The parable of talents (Matthew 25:14-30) shows that God entrusts to different people different amounts of money and that the reward for gaining two talents was the same as for gaining five talents (Matthew 25:21, 23). Jesus said that the widow who gave two mites gave more than those who gave from their abundance. The amount with which you have been entrusted is unimportant, but how you handle it is very important.[7] God never condemns wealth nor commends poverty. Whatever God chooses to entrust you with, hold with an open hand. "He who is faithful in what is least is faithful also in much..." (Luke 16:10).

4. **Money will never satisfy.** Solomon said, "He who loves silver will not be satisfied with silver; /Nor he who loves abundance, with increase. This also is vanity" (Ecclesiastes 5:10). If anyone should know it was Solomon, who was perhaps the richest man who ever lived. It is reported that someone once asked John D. Rockefeller, "How much money does it take to be satisfied?" His reply was "More."

   Jesus said, "...one's life does not consist in the abundance of the things he possesses..." He then told the parable of the rich man whose land brought forth plentifully. Was the rich man satisfied? No. He wanted to pull down his barns and build bigger ones. Then he thought he would have security and satisfaction. God called this man, as well as anyone who would lay up treasure for himself, a fool (Luke 12:15-21). Some of the most miserable people on earth are those who have secured wealth and once thought that money and possessions would satisfy.

5. **Priorities**. "But seek first the kingdom of God and His righteousness, and all these things shall be added to you"

(Matthew 6:33). Your number one key for a more prosperous life is to make God number one in all you do. Your order of priority should be the following: 1) God, 2) spouse, if any, 3) children, if any, 4) church, 5) friends, 6) vocation and 7) money.[8] A story is told of some boys who planned to slip into a store at night and change all the price tags so that items that were very valuable would have price tags of only a few cents while inexpensive items would have high prices. This is an illustration of the way some people have their values mixed up.[9]

6. **Wealth.** Nowhere in the scripture does it state it is a sin to be wealthy. Abram had so many flocks, herds, and tents that the land was not able to bear both Abram and Lot, for their substance was great (Genesis 13:5-6). Yet of him it is said, "Abraham believed God and it was accounted to him for righteousness" (Romans. 4:3). Boaz was described as "a man of great wealth" (Ruth 2:1). This man functioned as a kinsman redeemer and was a type of Jesus Christ. Job was called "the greatest of all the people of the East," yet God called him a perfect and upright man (Job. 1:1-3). After his trial, "the LORD blessed the latter days of Job more than his beginning" (Job 42:12). Also, the Lord gave Solomon both riches and honor so that there would be no king like unto him all his days (I Kings 3:13). The ability to earn wealth is given by God (Deuteronomy 8:18). Scripture implies that wrong attitudes toward money, such as the love of it, greed, and covetousness are the sins, rather than prosperity itself. In fact, God is the author of prosperity. "Beloved, I pray that you may prosper in all things and be in health, just as your soul prospers" (III John 2). "This Book of the Law shall not depart from your mouth, but you shall meditate in it day and night, that you may observe to do according to all that is written in it. For then you will make your way prosperous, and then you will have good success" (Joshua 1:8). "Praise the LORD! Blessed is the man who fears the LORD, /Who delights greatly in His commandments. His descendants will be mighty on earth; /The generation of the upright will be

blessed. Wealth and riches will be in his house, /And his righteousness endures forever" (Psalm 112:1-3). God, in general, seems to want his children to prosper so that his work shall prosper. It does not seem to be wrong to ask that God would bless and prosper every church, missionary endeavor, and Bible college operating in His will.

7. **Better than money.** There are many things much better than money, such as, the fear of the Lord, a dinner of herbs where love is, righteousness, wisdom, understanding, a humble spirit, a dry morsel with quietness, walking in integrity, and a good name (Proverbs 15:16, 17; 16:8, 16, 19; 17:1; 19:1; 22:1). I could add to this list other things that are worth more than money, such as knowing God, respect for the Lord, obedience to God's laws, relationships, kindness, knowing right and wrong, God's blessing, good sense, and fairness.[10] A number of Christians were asked to list what they consider to be true riches. They listed Jesus Christ, family, friends, helping others, feeling loved, having important work to do, health, a happy home, peace, joy, positive attitude, harmony, common sense, contentment, faith, and hope.[11]

8. **A proper attitude.** Jesus said to lay up treasures in heaven because where your treasure is, there will be your heart also (Matthew 6:19-21). Paul said to, "Set your mind on things above, not on things on the earth" (Colossians 3:2). Many Christians have missed the blessings of God while amassing their fortunes on earth. "Do not overwork to be rich; /Because of your own understanding, cease!" (Proverbs 23:4). Jesus also said you can't serve both God and mammon. Many who have made money their god and master have ended up as shipwrecks. "Remove falsehood and lies far from me; /Give me neither poverty nor riches; /Feed me with the food allotted to me; /Lest I be full and deny You, /And say, "Who is the LORD?" /Or lest I be poor and steal, /And profanc the name of my God" (Proverbs 30:8-9). I think what Agur, the writer of Proverbs 30, desired was to be what we call "middle class." He didn't want to be so rich that

he forgot God or be in poverty where he would be tempted to steal.

9. **Contentment.** Paul said, "Godliness with contentment is great gain" and "having food and clothing, with these we shall be content" (I Timothy 6:6, 8). Also he said, "I have learned in whatever state I am, to be content" (Philippians 4:11). Advertisers spend billions to sow seeds of discontent. Refuse to focus on what you don't have! It's time to be thankful rather than be depressed by a negative press. "Contentment is realizing that God has provided everything I need for my present circumstances."[12] "Better is a little with the fear of the LORD, /Than great treasure with trouble" (Proverbs 15:16).

   The following points can help you be more content:

   A. List your blessings.

   B. Take time to enjoy what God has given you.

   C. Develop an attitude of gratitude.

   D. Thank God for the difficult. "In everything give thanks; for this is the will of God ... " (I Thessalonians 5:18). Even in financial difficulties thank God that patience has a chance to grow.

   E. Share your blessings with others. Write a letter of thanks, make a phone call, send a gift, or visit face-to-face.[13]

10. **Covetousness.** Avoid playing the comparison game. The Bible calls it "coveting," we call it "keeping up with the Joneses."[14] The law told us not to covet anything that belongs to our neighbor (Exodus 20:17). This is confirmed in the New Testament (Romans 7:7, 13:9). The psalmist almost slipped when he became envious of the prosperity of others (Psalm 73:2-3). "Take heed and beware of covetousness, for one's life does not consist in the abundance of things he possesses" (Luke 12:15).

11. **Greediness.** "He who is greedy for gain troubles his own house" (Proverbs 15:27).

12. **The love of money.** The Bible does not say that money is the root of all evil but rather that "the love of money is the root of all evil" (I Timothy 6:10 KJV).[15] There is nothing wrong with money itself; what is wrong is the love of money. The poor, as well as the rich, can allow the love of money to cause them to commit all sorts of evil.

13. **Trusting in riches.** Our forefathers put on all our coins the words "In God We Trust" not "In Money We Trust." The problem the rich young ruler had was that he trusted in his riches and could not leave them to follow Jesus (Mark 10:17-27). Paul told Timothy to "Command those who are rich in this present age not to be haughty, nor to trust in uncertain riches but in the living God, who gives us richly all things to enjoy" (I Timothy 6:17). Solomon said that riches make themselves wings and fly away as an eagle (Proverbs 23:5). Jesus said that thieves steal, and moths and rust corrupt treasures laid up on earth (Matthew 6:19). More than one monetary system has failed, and it is prophesied that it will happen at least once more (Revelation 18:17).

14. **Pride.** Avoid being too proud to admit your own financial mistakes. Pride goes before destruction (Proverbs 16:18). Never buy for show. This is called conspicuous consumption.

15. **Honesty.** "Dishonest scales are an abomination to the LORD, /But a just weight is His delight" (Proverbs 11:1). "Diverse weights, and diverse measures, /They are both alike, an abomination to the LORD" (Proverbs 20:10). Dishonest business practices are an abomination to the Lord. An example of this is using inaccurate scales when weighing or measuring a product. Make up your mind to always be honest.

16. **Diligence.** "He who has a slack hand becomes poor, /But the hand of the diligent makes rich. He who gathers in summer is a wise son; /He who sleeps in harvest is a son who causes shame" (Proverbs 10:4-5). "Wealth gained by dishonesty will be diminished, /But he who gathers by labor will

increase" (Proverbs 13:11). Avoid the temptation to think your money is going to manage itself. Most people who inherit large sums of money blow it. Be diligent and work hard. "All hard work brings a profit, but mere talk leads only to poverty" (Proverbs 14:23 NIV).

17. **Laziness.** A lazy person in Proverbs is called slothful or a sluggard. God disapproves of slothfulness. In the parable of the talents the one who did nothing with his talent was called a "wicked and slothful servant" and was cast into outer darkness (Matthew 25:14-30). The wicked servant knew he should have at least invested his talent with the money exchanger, but he did nothing and was punished. "The soul of a lazy man desires, and has nothing; /But the soul of the diligent shall be made rich" (Proverbs 13:4). A person must avoid the pitfalls of laziness (Proverbs 12:27). Laziness leads to hunger and to poverty (Proverbs 19:15, 20:4). The desire of the lazy man kills him because he refuses to labor (Proverbs 21:25). Paul said if any would not work he should not eat (II Thessalonians 3:10). It is very easy for a person to become lazy if there is no clock to punch or someone saying to go to work. We all should admit there is a little laziness in each of us and discipline ourselves to overcome this.[16]

18. **Drunkenness and loose living.** Drunkenness, gluttony, and prostitution all lead to poverty (Proverbs 6:26; 21:17; 23:20, 21, 29, 30).[17]

19. **Pay your bills on time.** "Do not withhold good from those to whom it is due, /When it is in the power of your hand to do so. Do not say to your neighbor, "Go, and come back, /And tomorrow I will give it," /When you have it with you" (Proverbs 3:27, 28). If you owe people money, pay them back as soon as possible. Also, if you have monthly payments, take care of them on time, not just to save interest, but because it is right.

20. **Cosigning.** Don't cosign another person's note (Proverbs 17:18). The reason a lending agency requires someone to cosign a note is they seriously question the borrower's ability

to pay off the loan. The biblical term for cosigning is "surety," which means being a guarantor for a debt. If you cosign the note and the original borrower is not able to pay, then you are liable to pay off the loan. Proverbs 22:27 states, "If you have nothing with which to pay, /Why should he take away your bed from under you?"[18] If you cosign a note, the lender could even take some of your possessions to pay off the note. A pastor of a church should never cosign a note for a member of the congregation. Otherwise, to avoid partiality, he would have to cosign for others also. This could result in a terrible financial mess.

21. **Instruction.** "Poverty and shame will come to him who disdains correction, /But he who regards a rebuke will be honored" (Proverbs 13:18). "Where there is no counsel, the people fall; /But in the multitude of counselors there is safety" (Proverbs 11:14). Seek as much counsel and advice as you can get. "A wise man listens to advice" (Proverbs 12:15 NIV). "Plans fail for lack of counsel, but with many advisors they succeed" (Proverbs 15:22 NIV). Also seek God's guidance.

22. **Wasting.** Proverbs 18:9 (KJV) states, "He also that is slothful in his work is brother to him that is a great waster." This scripture would indicate that both the person who does not use his energy to gain money and the person who wastes money are alike. There are many ways to prevent wasting money such as saving food leftovers and turning off the lights, air-conditioning and other electrical appliances when not in use. See Chapter 7 on "Stretching Your Dollars" for other ideas on how to eliminate waste.

23. **Get-rich-quick schemes.** "A man with an evil eye hastens after riches, /And does not consider that poverty will come upon him" (Proverbs 28:22). Pyramid and multilevel sales schemes have deceived many Christians. A Christian should not be involved in the lottery, or other forms of gambling. Gambling, sooner or later, always leads to financial ruin.[19] I don't know of any Christians who play the lottery, but I have

met some that continually seem to be waiting on lawsuits to make them wealthy. "Dishonest money dwindles away, but he who gathers money little by little makes it grow" (Proverbs 13:11 NIV).

24. **Plan ahead by saving.** A sensible person watches for problems ahead and prepares to meet them. You can expect some unforeseen financial emergencies (roof leaks, tires going bald, auto repairs). "The wise man saves for the future, but the foolish man spends whatever he gets" (Proverbs 21:20 TLB).

25. **Gather all the facts.** Before making a major financial decision, make sure you have gathered all the facts. "He who answers before listening-- that is his folly and his shame" (Proverbs 18:13 NIV). Don't believe everything you are told (Proverbs 14:15). Not everyone is honest.

26. **Know the value of what you sell.** When your price is fair, do not allow someone to beat your price down (Proverbs 20:14).

27. **Holding back wages.** The Lord hears the cries of the laborers who work in the fields and have their wages held back by fraud. Miseries will come upon employers who live in luxury at the expense of the employees (James 5:1-6).

28. **Treatment of the poor and unfortunate.** "He who oppresses the poor to increase his riches, /And he who gives to the rich, will surely come to poverty" (Proverbs 22:16). Throughout the scriptures, God has had concern for orphans and widows. The gleanings of the fields were to be left for them. Ruth, for example, gleaned in the fields of Boaz (Ruth 2:2-23). One of the aspects of pure religion is, "to visit orphans and widows in their trouble" (James 1:27). Paul exhorts us to do good, be rich in good works, ready to give, and willing to share (I Timothy 6:18). Be generous. However, it is better to teach a man how to fish than it is to give him a fish. "Give, and it will be given to you" (Luke 6:38).

29. **You can't take it with you.** Egyptian Pharaohs, as well as many others, have buried their treasures in their tombs, only to have these treasures stolen by thieves. They certainly did not take it with them into eternity. Others have been buried in their Cadillacs only to have the Cadillacs rust out with time. I have never, though, heard of a hearse pulling a U-Haul trailer, for it wouldn't do the dead man any good. Paul said, "We brought nothing into this world, and it is certain we can carry nothing out" (I Timothy 6:7). Job said, "Naked I came from my mother's womb, /And naked shall I return there. The LORD gave, and the LORD has taken away; /Blessed be the name of the LORD" (Job 1:21). In referring to a rich man, Solomon said, "As he came from his mother's womb, naked shall he return, /To go as he came; /And he shall take nothing from his labor /Which he may carry away in his hand" (Ecclesiastes 5:15). No wonder Jesus said to lay up treasures in heaven rather than on earth (Matthew 6:19, 20). Earthly treasures you will not take with you, but good deeds that you have done will be rewarded.

God's principles of finance are not dependent on the economy or how much money we do or do not have.[20] The principles mentioned in this book apply to people of all economic levels.

---

[1] Blue, 19.

[2] Burkett, *The Complete Financial Guide for Young Couples*, 24.

[3] Burkett, *Your Finances in Changing Times*, 40.

[4] Blue, 17-20.

[5] Burkett, *The Complete Financial Guide for Young Couples*, 8.

[6] Blue, 21.

[7] Ibid., 22.

[8] Galloway, 100-101.

[9] Campolo, Tony, *Who Switched The Price Tags?*, Word Publishing, Dallas, 1986, 13-14.

[10] Ibid., 129-130.

[11] Ibid., 95-96.

[12] *Character Sketches From the Pages of Scripture, Vol III,* First Edition, Institute In Basic Youth Conflicts, Inc., Rand McNally and Company, 1985, 78.

[13] Ibid., 102-105.

[14] Ibid., 80-81.

[15] Anderson, Douglas, Jr., *Owe No Man Anything*, Light & Salt, Route 1, Box 252, Hampshire, ix.

[16] Galloway, 78-79.

[17] Ibid., 79-80.

[18] Ibid., 83.

[19] Ibid., 82.

[20] Burkett, *Your Finances in Changing Times*, 13.

Chapter 5 - Goal Setting

Most of us are responders rather than planners. Statistics claim that less than 3% of Americans have written goals.[1] Financial planning is allocating limited financial resources among various unlimited alternatives.[2] Planning is thinking ahead and avoiding problems. Today's decisions determine destiny. Better decision making occurs when one considers the long-term perspective. If you do a good job managing what you have, you will be given more (Luke 19:26).

What short-term uses are there for income?

Income can be given away, spent to support a lifestyle, used for repayment of debt, used to meet tax obligations, or accumulated or saved. Your commitments and your priorities will determine how you use your money.[3]

Why should a couple thoroughly discuss finances before marriage?

There is no area of family relationships that demands more communication and cooperation than the area of finances. Living without a financial plan is like building a house without blueprints. Failing to plan is planning to fail.

Since financial problems are a common reason for divorce, couples need to discuss finances honestly and thoroughly before marriage. The marriage should be postponed until this is done. Many people look upon marriage as a solution to all economic woes. You should realize that your spouse's earning power might never be much greater than it is when you marry, since education or professional training usually determines this. Before marriage, a couple should decide if they would be able to live on one income after they have children. There is probably nothing that can make a couple more miserable than to be continually dissatisfied with their standard of living. The fact that money is never going to make you happy should be understood before you get married.[4] Different backgrounds can have an enormous impact on a marriage. Since opposites often attract, many couples have differences with regard to the time of going to bed, sense of direction, messiness, and in the area of finances. For example, one may desire to live within a budget, while the other sees this as very restrictive. One may be frugal, while the other is an impulsive spender.[5] One may be a good record keeper, while the other has never kept records. It is doubtful that the personality of either partner will change, so, if a marriage is to work, these differences should be considered prior to marriage, lest you become combatants rather than companions.[6] Differences can be used to complement one another, rather than as a source of contention.

What else should a couple know or do before marriage?

1. Attend a good pre-marital counseling class together.

2. Know how to balance a checkbook (See Appendix A).

3. Know how to budget (See Chapter 6). Write down goals before you're married, including the first year's budget. Plan one day each year to get away and review your budget.[7]

4. Both parties should be out of debt.

5. Have enough saved to pay for the honeymoon and two to three month's expenses.

6. Be able to afford housing separately from parents. If you are not able to leave you should not cleave (Genesis 2:24).

What are some long-term objectives for savings?

1. Major purchases (appliances, automobile, house, etc.).

2. Financial independence.

3. College education for children. The cost of a college education is increasing faster than the inflation rate. Many are saving money by going to a Bible college or a community college for two years before going to a university. One should also investigate work programs, scholarships and grants.[8]

4. Major lifestyle change.

5. Major charitable giving.

6. Owning your own business.[9]

7. Retirement.

8. Passing on an inheritance.

How can a person be financially successful?

If you spend less than you earn, and continue doing this for a long period of time, you will be financially successful. "He who gathers money little by little makes it grow" (Proverbs 13:11 NIV). Another way to say this is that most people who achieve wealth get rich slowly. For example, if at age twenty you saved $1,000/year and invested it at 12.5%, at age sixty you would have $1,000,000, while if at age forty you saved $10,000/year and invested at 12.5% at age sixty you would have $1,000,000.[10] In the first example one would save $40,000 to reach $1,000,000. The second, however, would have to save $200,000 to reach $1,000,000. The earlier you start, and the more you earn in interest and dividends, the less you need to start with. Only $2.74 per day is needed to save $1,000/year. Appendix B shows how to calculate how money grows.

The above figures do not take into account taxes, but they can be deferred in an Individual Retirement Account (IRA). Better yet, use a pre-tax retirement deduction. Also, due to inflation the $1,000,000 will not have the purchasing power forty years from now that it does today. This is true, but $0 purchases the same now, as it will then.

How can you easily save this amount without much sacrificing?

Instead of going out to eat two or three times per week, you could enjoy a steak at home. However, probably the best place to save is the family car. People who hold on to their cars for at least ten years, rather than trading every three years, can save $400,000 to $450,000 over forty years, even counting an older car's higher maintenance costs. That savings alone could enable most people to retire five years earlier than those who trade in their cars every three years.[11]

How can one approximate how money will grow?

The "magic of compounding" can be approximated by "The Rule of 72," which states that if you divide 72 by the interest rate (or rate of return), expressed as a percent, you will determine the approximate number of years it takes to double your money.[12] For example, at 9% interest it will take approximately eight years (72 divided by 9 = 8) to double your money. If you invested $10,000 at 9%, after eight years it would increase to $20,000, after sixteen years it would increase to $40,000, and after twenty-four years it would increase to $80,000. Consider the following table:

Interest rate or rate of return %	Rule of 72 Approximate Number of years to double	Rule of 72 Approximate Multiplication rate in 36 years	Approximate Value of investment of $10,000 after 36 years
2	36	2	$20,000
4	18	4	$40,000
6	12	8	$80,000
8	9	16	$160,000
12	6	64	$640,000

The table above and the graph "How Money Grows" in Chapter 13 show how important it is to obtain a good interest rate (or rate of return) if you want your money to grow rapidly.

How can a person reach long-term financial goals?

In order to reach your long-term goals you have to make your long-term goals a priority over your short-term goals. This is sometimes called delayed gratification. To achieve long-term financial goals will require substantial financial resources and without an inheritance or striking oil, the only way to accumulate is to spend less than you earn and invest the difference. A positive cash flow (earning more than you spend) is absolutely essential if you are to accomplish either long-term or short-term financial objectives. Margin is the difference between what you earn and what you spend. So how do you increase your margin? To fund an increase through increasing earnings also requires funding the taxes and the tithes. Thus, a dollar earned is not a dollar saved. Besides this, increasing earning is very difficult without taking a second job and this often is contrary to other goals, such as spending more time with your family. The best way to increase margin is to cut spending. Recognize that every dollar saved in the living expense category goes directly to the cash flow margin. A dollar saved now puts multiple dollars in the future. So where do you cut? Tithes should not be cut. Taxes can't be cut.[13]

In order to generate margin, the only truly discretionary place to cut spending is in the area of lifestyle. Living a consumptive lifestyle is probably the biggest mistake you can make if you wish to achieve your financial goals. It is difficult to avoid excessive spending because there is no worldly support and very little Christian support. Advertising is extremely sophisticated and effective. It has been shown that the more TV a person watches, and the more time a person spends in malls, the higher the desired lifestyle.[14]

What are some reasons that goals are vital?

Goals provide direction and purpose. Otherwise circumstances, people, or feelings determine our actions.

1. Goals help us crystallize our thinking.

2. Goals provide personal motivation.

3. Goals are statements of God's will for me. "The Lord willing, I plan to achieve the following." Otherwise, goals are a presumption (James 4:13-15). Paul said, "I press toward the goal" (Philippians 3:14).

What are some barriers to goal setting?

1. We consider ourselves failures if we don't reach the goals we set.

2. We assume that it takes a lot of time to set goals.

3. We don't know what goals to set.

4. We don't know how to set goals.[15]

How does one go about setting faith goals?

1. Consider God's will when setting your faith goals. Spend time with God. Pray about your goals to be sure they are the right ones. When money becomes your focus, you are

doomed to disappointment because money is merely a resource. The gaining of wealth as an end in itself is a very poor investment. It can be to the exclusion of everything else, such as family, friends, hobbies, and relaxation. There is no correlation between wealth and happiness.[16] You do not test God by dreaming up goals. Rather you should spend time with Him and be assured your goals are His will.

2. Record the impressions no matter how impossible they may seem.

   A. The means of accomplishment may not be evident. Noah probably had no idea how he was going to build such a huge ark, but he kept at it (Genesis 6).

   B. You often start with inadequate resources. Sarah was barren and past childbearing age when God gave her a goal to be a mother. Certainly the disciples did not know how Jesus was going to feed the multitude with five barley loaves and two small fish (John 6).

   C. The goals may not be fully understood. Abraham didn't know where he was going when God called him to go to a place he would later receive as an inheritance (Hebrews 11:8).

3. Make the goals measurable. Objectives are broad purposes, such as providing for family, advancing the cause of Christ, and becoming financially independent. Goals are measurable, accomplishable, specific things. Write down your short-term financial goals (1-year). Write down your intermediate financial goals (5 years). Write down your long-term financial goals (20 years). Perhaps start your goals with a sentence such as, "By _____(date) I hope to see the following take place." In a husband/wife situation do not set goals apart from or in disagreement with your spouse.

4. Give God the flexibility to do things His way, with His timing, and His resources. Don't set the goals in concrete.[17] Goals are a guideline but should not control one's life. Even

Jesus had his plan to go to Jairus' house temporarily interrupted by the woman with the issue of blood.

What are some steps to financial advancement?

1. Visualize where you want to go: In 5 years, 10 years and 20 years.

2. Work your plan.

   A. Tithe.

   B. Pay taxes and bills.

   C. Save.

   D. Live on the rest.

3. Commit to the task of moving ahead financially.

4. Begin now.

5. Deny the lesser to gain the greater.[18] Financial maturity is being able to give up today's desires for tomorrow's benefits. There is a price to be paid for the best things in life. You must pay the price of self-discipline to be financially free, but it's worth it to avoid financial problems.

On a regular basis, you need to take an honest look at where you are financially, in order to see how you are progressing toward your financial goals. Each month you should balance your checkbook. On an annual basis you should prepare and review a statement of net worth. You determine your net worth by listing assets and totaling their values and listing liabilities (debts) and totaling their values. Your net worth is the difference between your assets and your liabilities. If the result is negative, you are in big trouble. Your first major goal, while providing for your family, probably will be to get out of debt. If you see that you are not progressing toward your financial goals, you probably need to review your budget and make some changes.

A mountain is climbed one step at a time. Likewise, financial goals are achieved one step at a time.[19]

[1] Blue, 99.

[2] Ibid., 26.

[3] Ibid., 27.

[4] Burkett, *The Complete Financial Guide for Young Couples*, 18.

[5] Burkett, Larry, *Answers To Your Family's Financial Questions*, Focus on the Family Publishing, 1987, 21.

[6] Burkett, *The Complete Financial Guide for Young Couples*, 21, 22.

[7] Burkett, *Answers To Your Family's Financial Questions*, 36.

[8] Ibid., 144.

[9] Blue, 29.

[10] Ibid., 35, 36.

[11] Rankin, Deborah, "Start Now Retire Early," Reader's Digest, Reader's Digest Association, Inc., Pleasantville, NY, February 1998, 101.

[12] Ibid., 36.

[13] Ibid., 40.

[14] Ibid., 113, 114.

[15] Ibid., 99-101.

[16] Burkett, *Your Finances in Changing Times*, 42.

[17] Blue, 102-108.

[18] Galloway, 122-124.

[19] Ibid., 47.

Chapter 6 - Budgeting

What is a budget and how can it help you?

Simply put, a budget is a plan of how you will spend your money. Some prefer to call a budget a spending plan because the term budget is a "bitter pill" for some to swallow.[1,2] Without a budget you are, in reality, living as a responder rather than a planner. Only a small percentage of people have enough money or make enough money that they don't need to budget.[3] A budget is a programmed guidance system to keep us on target and assure us of reaching our financial goals. The majority of people do not get into financial difficulty because of emergency situations (car wreck, medical bills, leaky roof, etc.) but rather by default (Proverbs 22:3). The budget is designed to help not hurt, free not enslave, give you the best and not deprive you. Though we often view making a living by a budget as constraining, it can be the most financially freeing thing we can do. A budget will help you get out of debt and can be used to develop good communication between husband and wife.[4] A budget must work for the entire family and not just one person.

How can a person grasp the concept of budgeting?

Budgeting seems to be a difficult concept for some to grasp. First, let us consider a simple cash only budget for Jim, a fifteen-year-old teenager who lives at home and has most of his expenses provided. At the start of the year his parents decide to teach him the principles of budgeting when they start giving him his allowance of $50.00 per month. He will be responsible for four categories of his expenses: his contributions, eating outside the home, recreation and gifts. Jim decides on a spending plan (budget) for the month as follows: Contributions-$7.00, Eating Out-$20.00, Recreation-$20.00 and Gifts-$3.00. He gets four envelopes, writes the name of each category on the separate envelope, and puts the budgeted amount in each envelope. Then, as he spends, Jim writes down the amounts on the appropriate envelope.

For example, in the Eating Out category, he spends the following in the first three weeks: $6.00, $7.00, and $5.00. His envelope would look as follows:

Category	Eating Out
Amount budgeted	20 00
Amounts spent	6 00
	7 00
	5 00
Total spent	
Balance at End of Month	

He now has only $2.00 left in this category. Theoretically, when he runs out of money in the envelope, he should quit spending in that category. In the fourth week, Jim is asked to go out to eat after church. He has several choices. One is to refuse to go out; another is to just order a soda or something else that costs less than $2.00. A third choice, which is least desirable, is to borrow from another category. Jim chooses to go out and orders only a soda which, including taxes and tip, costs $1.25. Thus, at the end of the month he has $0.75 left in the envelope.

His envelope for the Eating Out category would now look as follows:

Category	Eating Out
Amount budgeted	20 00
Amounts spent	6 00
	7 00
	5 00
	1.25
Total Spent	19 25
Balance at End of Month.	0.75

In his other categories, Jim gives the entire $7.00 of his Contributions, spends $15.00 on Recreation, and spends nothing on Gifts. Thus, he has nothing to carry over in Contributions, but has balances of $0.75 in Eating Out, $5.00 in Recreation, and $3.00 in Gifts at the end of the month. These are called carry-overs.

On February 1, he receives another $50.00 as allowance. He can choose to keep the same spending plan or alter it. Since he has spent nothing on Gifts, he may think he can eliminate this category. However, he remembers that this coming year he will have to pay for the gifts that he gives, and he will need at least $36.00 for Christmas. So he decides to leave this category alone and let it build up. Also, he recalls how short he was in the Eating Out category. But he also knows that he would like to go skiing in February or March, which will cost $40.00. He is tempted to cut his contributions but, after praying about it, does not think this is right. So he leaves all the categories as they were and decides to put the same amount in each envelope as he did the month before. He gets four new envelopes for February, which now look as follows:

Month	February		Month	February
Category	Contribution		Category	Eating Out
Carry over from Jan	0 00		Carry over from Jan	0 75
Budgeted for Feb	7.00		Budgeted for Feb	20.00
New Balance	7.00		New Balance	20.75

Month	February		Month	February
Category	Recreation		Category	Gifts
Carry over from Jan	5 00		Carry over from Jan	3 00
Budgeted for Feb	20.00		Budgeted for Feb	3.00
New Balance	25.00		New Balance	6.00

On February 2, he finds out that the ski trip will be on February 20. Jim decides to cut down his Eating Out and borrow $15.00 from this category so he can go skiing.

At the end of the month these two envelopes look as follows:

Month	February		Month	February
Category	Eating Out		Category	Recreation
Carry over from Jan	0 75		Carry over from Jan	5 00
Budgeted for Feb	20.00		Budgeted for Feb	20.00
New Balance	20 75		New Balance	25 00
Amounts Spent	1 25		Amounts Spent	40 00
	1 25			
	1.25			
Total Spent	3 75		Total Spent	40 00
Balance at end of month	17 00		Balance at end of month	(15 00)

You will note that he has a negative balance for the Recreation budget. Jim decides to keep the same spending plan for March because he realizes that he does not go skiing every month. He puts the same amount in each envelope as he has the previous months and then takes $15.00 out of the Recreation envelope and puts it in the Eating Out envelope in order to pay back what he has borrowed. His March envelopes for Eating Out and Recreation would look as follows:

Month	March
Category	Eating Out
Carry over from Feb	17 00
Budgeted for Mar	20.00
New Balance	37 00
Amounts Spent	
Total Spent	
Balance at end of month	

Month	March
Category	Recreation
Carry over from Feb	(15 00)
Budgeted for Mar	20.00
New Balance	5 00
Amounts Spent	
Total Spent	
Balance at end of month	

You will note that Jim has $5.00 to spend for recreation in March unless he "borrows" again. If he sees that he consistently needs more money in certain categories he may have to change his spending plan. After a year or so of sticking with his budget, Jim's parents may decide to increase his allowance and make him responsible for other items, such as clothing. If Jim feels he needs more money than his parents can supply, he may need to get a part-time job to provide extra income. Other suggestions regarding money and children are included in Appendix C.

A family or a person living away from home has additional categories of expenses as shown below. Also, instead of cash, many expenses will be paid with checks or a credit card. Instead of recording expenditures on a set of envelopes, they will be recorded on a form as shown in Appendix D or into a budgeting program on a computer. The principle, however, is just the same as using the envelopes.

What must a person do to start budgeting?

1. Find out how much money comes in from every source. This includes salary, commissions, tips, interest, dividends, bonuses, gifts, and other income.[5]

2. Categorize your expenditures to determine how much money you are spending and in what areas.[6] It is difficult to have your finances under control without keeping good records and understanding the basics of good bookkeeping.

Otherwise, you won't even know how much you are spending.

How can you estimate how much you will budget for each category?

The best way to estimate how much you spend in each category is to go through the past twelve months of your checkbook and credit card statements and average the amount spent in each category per month. If you have a computer, there are some good programs to assist you in this task. To track cash expenditures, you must write down what you purchased and how much you spent each time you spend. Otherwise, you won't remember where your money went. Break down these cash expenditures and add them to the totals from your check and credit card records.

What are some typical categories for a family budget?

1. Contributions (tithes, offerings, faith promise, etc.).

2. Housing expenses other than utilities (mortgage or rent, insurance, maintenance, repairs, and furnishings).

3. Utilities (oil, electricity, gas, water, sewage, and garbage).

4. Food, cash and miscellaneous.

5. Clothing (including cleaning and alterations).

6. Communications (telephone, postage, stationery, and Internet access).

7. Transportation (auto payments, gasoline, repairs, insurance, bus fares, and cost of rides).

8. Medical, including dental.

9. Gifts, books, magazines, and newspapers.

10. Recreation, travel, and entertainment.

11. Life insurance.

12. Education.

13. Extra taxes (personal property, real estate, etc.).

14. Savings.

15. Debt repayment (for those currently in debt).

How can a person implement a budget?

1. Compare your income with your expenditures, making sure of the following:

    A. Your contributions are equal to or greater than 10% of your gross income.

    B. All fixed payments, such as mortgage and life insurance, are budgeted.

    C. Your top priorities, such as education and annual vacation, are included.

2. Adjust your totals so that your budgeted expenses are equal to or less than your income, even if it means selling the extra car, moving into a smaller house, etc. Every successful budget has income that exceeds expenditures. Except perhaps for house payments, you should endeavor to get out of debt as quickly as possible .

3. Get an accountant's pad with thirteen columns and head each column with the categories that are applicable to you. A typical budget sheet will look like the one in Appendix D. The amounts that you plan to spend for each category should be out on the line called "budgeted for this month." You may not need to use columns for life insurance if this is paid on an annual basis, or for extra taxes if they are not paid too often, or savings which can be kept track of in a savings passbook or other investment vehicle. These categories, however, still must be budgeted for, even though a column is not allotted.

4. Keep a record of all expenditures. This can be done easily if most expenditures are paid by check.

5. Balance your checkbooks monthly, as soon as you get your bank statement. (See Appendix A).

6. At the end of each month enter the amounts spent in each category on the budget sheet, total these figures and see what balance you have. Then transfer the balance at the end to the "carryover" on a new sheet for a new pay period.

7. Allow some accounts to build up as a cushion "saving up for a rainy day." In this way you will have funds for household maintenance and medical expenses that do not occur each month.

8. Live within the budget. Do not charge non-budgeted items, even if it means eating beans until the next paycheck. If there is not enough income to meet your allocated expenses, you must cut back on spending no matter what. If you are behind in your payments, you should write your creditors sending a copy of your budget. Use any additional income, such as the sale of assets, salary increases, bonuses, etc. to retire debts. Realize it will take months to correct the situation. It's a lot of fun to get into debt, but not much fun to get out of debt. This requires discipline.[7]

What are some common budget errors to be avoided?

1. Don't go to extremes. You can't cut food out of your budget! Some other things also are necessities.

2. Beware of increasing your spending when your income increases. Pregnancy or layoffs can stop temporary income. In the case of a couple, save the wife's income for one-time purchases, such as a car, down payment on a home, or a vacation.

3. Don't think "a little debt won't hurt."

4. Avoid automatic overdrafts.

5. Avoid automatic tellers unless you are very careful to write each transaction in your checkbook.

6. Balance your checkbook each month down to the penny.

7. Don't give up. Be aware that the most common cause of budget failure is discouragement. STICK WITH IT!

8. Don't forget to budget for auto repairs, clothing, and dental and medical expenses.[8] Realize there are very few unexpected expenses.

Spend only what you allocate. Poverty and shame will come to him who neglects discipline (Proverbs 13:18 NIV). The biggest violations of a budget usually occur when big-ticket items, such as boats and automobiles are purchased.

Your family can afford vacations if you budget month by month and put the money aside. You can, however, reduce costs by taking a camping vacation and renting a tent or camp trailer rather than staying in motels.[9]

If you don't overspend, you won't get in debt.

---

[1] How to Manage Your Financial Resources: Creating a Spending Plan You Can Control, The Institute of Certified Financial Planners, 1996, 3.

[2] Galloway, 71.

[3] Burkett, *The Complete Financial Guide for Young Couples*, 30.

[4] Burkett, *Answers To Your Family's Financial Questions*, 47, 49.

[5] How to Manage Your Financial Resources, 2.

[6] Burkett, *Answers To Your Family's Financial Questions*, 50.

[7] Ibid., 56-57.

[8] Ibid., 58-60.

[9] Ibid., 67.

Chapter 7 – Getting Out Of Debt and Staying Out

What is debt?

Debt is any money owed to anyone for anything.[1] Others modify this to say that you are in debt when you can't pay what you promised.[2] You must pay back what you have borrowed plus interest. If you borrow money and spend today, you are going to have to sacrifice doubly in order to repay it in the days, months, and sometimes years ahead.

One must contrast what the Bible teaches with what is taught in business schools. The idea of using other people's money develops a credit mentality that allows people to buy what they cannot afford to own.[3] The plumb line for truth, however, is God's word, not a college textbook or standard practice.

The Bible discourages the use of debt but does not prohibit it. However, there is not one positive reference in the entire Bible for borrowing money.[4] Debt is never the real problem; rather, it is symptomatic of the real problem, which may be greed, self-indulgence, impatience, fear, poor self-esteem, lack of self-worth, or lack of self-discipline.[5] When a Christian continues to borrow without the means to repay, his attitude falls into the category of deceit and greed, never willing to sacrifice, never willing to deny his impulse. "He who loves pleasure will be a poor man" (Proverbs 21:17).

What excuses are sometimes used to justify going into debt?

1. Buy now; it will cost more later. This idea supposes that everything increases in price. However, in the last few years, computers and oil have dropped in price. The following are the real criteria: "Do I need it?" and "Can I afford it?" Better decisions are usually made when one pays cash rather than purchasing on credit. The real question is not what it costs; the real question is whether it is a need or greed? God will supply needs (Philippians 4:19). There is a difference between needs and wants.

2. If you borrow to buy, you will be paying off the debt with cheaper dollars. This assumes that the rate of inflation will be greater than the rate of interest. However, over the past 700 years the average annual rate of interest charged for loans has been approximately 3% greater than the average inflation rate. Thus, by being on the borrowing side of inflation you will always lose to inflation because you will have the magic of compounding working against you.

3. You can never accumulate enough.[6] If you can't afford to pay cash now, how can you afford to pay cash plus interest? Some have asked, "Is it wise to borrow for appreciating assets?" First of all, you don't know if the asset is going to continue to appreciate. Houses were formerly thought to be appreciating assets, but in some parts of the country, such as in Houston, the value of housing dropped by half in the mid-1980's. In reality, most families have to borrow to buy a house, but they should commit to pay off the loan as soon as possible.[7]

What are some dangers of debt?

Insurance companies say that those heavily in debt are accident-prone. Also, it has been determined that those with oppressive debts are not as productive in their work. Debt is discouraging and can be a divisive issue in a family. Sales presentations are so alluring and payment plans are made to look so easy that you can fall into the debt trap and be caught almost before you know it.[8] The following are some other dangers of debt.

1. **The economic danger of debt** is simply that you pay more for everything you purchase on credit. Compounding works against you. The following chart shows the huge difference between what you think you pay and what you actually pay when you purchase on credit. Notice what you will pay for a 30-year mortgage for $100,000 on a home at 8% interest.

Borrowed	$100,000
Interest rate	8%
360 Monthly payments at	$734
Total payments	$264,155

You actually pay over two and one-half times what you borrow.

The next chart shows what you pay when you borrow at 11.0% interest to purchase a car.

New car loan	$10,000.00
48 monthly payments at	258.50
Amount paid	$12,408.00

As you can see, you pay almost $2,500 more for the car by borrowing to purchase this car than if you paid cash for it.

2. **Debt becomes a trap**, which in some cases, is nearly impossible to get out of. Realization comes when the glamour of whatever was purchased has worn off, and the money needed to repay the debt prevents you from buying other things.

For example, suppose a couple overspends $1,000 per year for ten years and realizes they are in debt for $10,000. Not only do they have to repay $10,000, but also the interest, which amounts to $1,500/year at a 15% interest rate. In order to net enough to pay the $11,500, they will have to earn considerably more because of taxes and tithes.

3. **Debt always mortgages the future.** Although you may temporarily enjoy a higher standard of living, in the long term you may actually reduce your standard of living.[9]

What are some spiritual dangers of debt?

1. **You may be disobeying Romans 13:8** which states, "Owe no one anything except to love one another." Many argue that this is taken out of context. I am not sure about this. Many translations, such as, "Pay all your debts except the debt of love for others" (LNT) indicate a financial application for this verse.

2. **Borrowing can produce bondage.** The borrower is servant to the lender (Proverbs 22:7). What is financial bondage? In the past, not paying one's debts was considered worse than stealing because a trust was violated. Debtors were even put in prison.[10, 11] Now there is mental bondage where you recognize you are in debt beyond your ability to repay. If I owe anything to someone I am not free to give love to that person. A wall immediately goes up as a result of debtor/lender relationship.

3. **Borrowing always presumes on the future** (James 4:13-16). If you do not have a guaranteed way to repay what you borrow, you are presuming upon the future. By taking on debt you may run the risk of not providing for your own, and anyone who does not provide for his household, "has denied the faith and is worse than an unbeliever" (I Timothy 5:8).

4. **Borrowing may prevent God from withholding harmful items.** "But those who desire to be rich fall into temptation and a snare, and into many foolish and harmful lusts which drown men in destruction and perdition" (I Timothy 6:9).

5. **Borrowing may deny God an opportunity to work**. God has promised to supply our needs. When we borrow we are putting the lender in the place of God. Why trust in God to provide for us if someone will lend to us? We seem unwilling to wait for God's timing. His ways are different from our ways (Isaiah 55:8, 9). If God wants us to have something, He will provide the funds in due time. God's work, done in God's way, will not lack God's support.

What are some biblical principles regarding borrowing?

"The wicked borrows and does not repay" (Psalms 37:21). Borrowing is making a vow that we must keep.

Proverbs makes numerous references to surety (guaranteeing the debt of another).[12] The references clearly indicate that guaranteeing the debt of another is not wise.[13]

How can a person avoid debt?

The best way to stay out of debt is to spend less than what you earn. Thus, you need a budget as described in chapter 6 and probably need to curtail your use of credit cards as described below. Perhaps you need to let the church know of a temporary financial need. Someone with a ministry of giving might be blessed to supply the need.

What about credit cards?

There is no doubt that credit cards, if used properly, can be very beneficial.

1. It is often almost impossible to rent a car without a credit card.

2. You can reserve motel rooms and airline tickets with a credit card.

3. In some places, credit cards are helpful in cashing or writing checks; however, all that is needed in some states is a valid driver's license with your photo on it.

4. Having a credit card enables you to carry less cash when traveling.

5. A credit card does provide a permanent record for business and tax purposes. Receipts for credit card purchases, as well as monthly statements, should be saved.

6. Some credit cards give perks, such as airline frequent flier miles, for each dollar spent.

However, the mere use of credit cards can cause a family to spend considerably more regardless of whether the full statement is paid off each month. You might look at all of your statements at the end of the year and see if there were any purchases that you would not have made if you had not had a credit card. With a credit card you are tempted to buy things you wouldn't if you had to spend cash or write a check and look at your balance. If you are using an oil company credit card for other than gasoline purchases you are probably paying too much. Things like oil, tires, batteries, and parts usually cost more at a service station than at a discount store or parts supply store. Even with gasoline, you often pay several cents more per gallon if you charge. Sometimes you can pay less for other items if you don't use a credit card. The retailer pays 2 1/2 to 5% on every credit card purchase. You might ask them if they would give you a discount if you would pay cash.[14]

There are other ways to establish credit without using credit cards. One way is by paying your utility bills in a prompt and complete way each month. You can use these utility companies as references. Another way of establishing credit is to put some item on lay-away and make regular payments. On lay-away, you don't get the goods until you make the final payment.[15]

Why do banks mail out billions of pre-approved credit card solicitations each year?

Credit cards are the banks' most profitable business. When banks can borrow money at 4% to 5% and loan it to card holders at 17%, they have little incentive to proceed cautiously even though credit card delinquencies have reached an all time high. Card-issuers are actively hunting for undisciplined spenders, who might carry large unpaid balances from month to month.[16, 17]

What rules should a person apply if they have credit cards?[18]

1. **Use only for budgeted items.**

2. **Pay off every month.** In the banking industry, a person who pays off his credit card each month is known as a "deadbeat" because the bank does not get to charge the 17-21% interest. Some card-issuers have even begun to levy an annual penalty on accounts paid in full.[19]

3. **Destroy your cards if you can't abide by Rules 1 and 2.** One person literally froze a credit card in a block of ice. It was then available only after a long period of melting and thinking.

What are some ways to get out of debt?[20]

1. **Recognize how much your heavy debt is costing you.**

   How do people get in debt?

   A. They use credit cards and don't pay the entire balance each month.

   B. They spend more than they make.

   C. They borrow for things, such as a vacation, that have little or no cash value left after the time of the expenditure .

2. **Determine to be debt-free.**

3. **Declare a moratorium on any additional debts.** If you don't borrow money, you can't get into debt. Getting out of debt is an uphill climb all the way.

4. **Cut up all credit cards and throw them away if you can't use them properly.** If you have a radical debt problem, it requires radical action.

5. **Sell some assets that are not absolutely necessary**, such as a truck, boat, or camper and use the funds to pay off some debts. Many cannot sell assets. Eighty percent of Americans owe more than what they own. Thus, there is the slow painful difficult process of monthly payments.[21] Before selling your home, consider what rent or the next home would cost.

6. **Set debt reduction goals** - as large as reasonable.

7. **Use all extra income, such as income tax refunds, raises, and bonuses, to pay off your depressing debts.**

8. **Get started right away.**

9. **Make whatever financial sacrifices are necessary to achieve your goal.** Use personal discipline to give up lesser things to achieve the greater goal of being debt free. Deny yourself instant gratification. Say no to impulsive buying.

10. **Be determined and don't give up.**

11. **Go directly to creditors with a plan.** Run toward those you owe rather than away from them (Matthew 5:25).[22]

Consolidation loans should only be used as a last resort since all they do is add all of your smaller debts together to make one large one. These loans don't pay off the debt any sooner. Before consolidating (combining) debts, develop a budget and live by it for six months; otherwise, you are treating the symptom and not the problem. Without a definite plan, consolidating previous loans into one loan with a smaller minimum payment will only open the door for further overspending. An equity loan usually has the best interest rate and is tax deductible; however, a home usually represents security and comfort, so, if you are married, pray about it with your spouse.[23] Another possibility is to borrow, at a low interest rate, against the cash value of your life insurance policy.

What should a person consider before going into debt?

Is the cost to borrow less than the economic benefit received? Only borrow money when what you borrow for has collateral, or it is going to make you money or save you money. Some think borrowing for an education may be good because it will increase your earning power. However, this assumes that you will be able to get a job when you graduate and have the ability to pay the loan off in the future. What if you become disabled? What if God would call you to home or foreign missionary work? It is far better to work your way through school or stay out for a year or so to save money. If you do borrow, shop around for the lowest interest rate and never borrow from someone that charges an excessive interest rate. Require and receive a truth-in-lending form from the lender. Remember every dollar you save on interest is another dollar you get to keep for yourself. A lower interest rate on debt can save you thousands of dollars.

What other questions should you ask before going into debt?

1. Is there a guaranteed way of repayment?

2. Are you and your spouse (if married) free from anxiety regarding this debt?

3. Do you have spiritual peace of mind?

4. Are there no other ways to meet these goals?

All investments and debts are presented as a good deal. However, the interest on credit card debts is too high, and consumer debt to finance cars, furniture, and vacations usually does not make sense economically. Even mortgage debt does not always meet the above criteria. You should not be so attached to the home you are buying that you couldn't give it up if the debt could not be paid. Investment and business debts have the same dangers as a personal debt. Many Christians operate their business debt free. If a business does borrow, the return must be greater than the cost.

All parties involved in paying off a debt must have unity. If any of the parties do not understand the debt, or feel uneasy about it, don't make the investment or obligate to the debt.[24]

What other suggestions should be considered regarding debt?

1. Usually, it is recommended to pay off your high interest debts first. However, it may be wise to pay off some small debts to show yourself that you are making progress. Even low-interest debts should be paid off. God wants his people to be debt free. No debt in Scripture exceeded seven years. If you pay off a home mortgage early you will save tremendously on interest.[25]

2. When you do pay off your debts, keep putting those monthly payments into a savings or money market account. Then the next time you make a major purchase you can pay cash for it and save a bundle in interest charges.

3. I don't believe that people should borrow for the Lord's work. I have heard of pastors asking saints to borrow money and give the money to build a church. God would not violate his word to accomplish his work.

4. Collateral is an asset pledged as security for a loan. If the loan is not paid, the asset reverts to the lender.[26] Collateral is required when the lender doubts that the borrower will be able to repay the loan. If there is a question regarding your ability to pay back the loan, you are violating one of the above-mentioned criteria for undertaking debt.

5. Automatic overdraft protection is not a good idea if it encourages people not to balance their checkbooks and creates automatic loans.[27]

6. Bankruptcy is not a way out for Christians. "The wicked borrows and does not repay, /But the righteous shows mercy and gives" (Psalms 37:21).[28]

[1] Blue, 55.

[2] Burkett, *Answers To Your Family's Financial Questions*, 118.

[3] Burkett, *The Complete Financial Guide for Young Couples*, 16.

[4] Ibid., 37.

[5] Blue, 55.

[6] Ibid., 48-51.

[7] Burkett, *Answers To Your Family's Financial Questions*, 128.

[8] Galloway, 51, 52.

[9] Blue, 56-59.

[10] Burkett, *Answers To Your Family's Financial Questions*, 115.

[11] Burkett, *Your Finances in Changing Times*, 54, 55.

[12] Burkett, *Answers To Your Family's Financial Questions*, 126.

[13] Blue, 60-63.

[14] MacGregor, Malcolm, *Your Money Matters*, Bethany Fellowship Inc., Minneapolis, MN, 88.

[15] Ibid., 88, 89.

[16] Hayes, Laurie, "Banks' Marketing Blitz Yields Rash of Defaults," The Wall Street Journal, September 25, 1996, B1, B6.

[17] Frank, Steven E., "Credit Card Delinquencies Increased to All-Time High at the End of 1996," The Wall Street Journal, March 14, 1997, A6.

[18] Burkett, *The Complete Financial Guide for Young Couples*, 39.

[19] Hayes, B1.

[20] Galloway, *55-64.*

[21] Blue, 121, 122.

[22] Burkett, *Answers To Your Family's Financial Questions*, 120.

[23] Ibid., 141-142.

[24] Blue, 64-68.

[25] Burkett, *Answers To Your Family's Financial Questions*, 124-125.

[26] Ibid., 129.

[27] Ibid., 130.

[28] Burkett, *Your Finances in Changing Times*, 130.

Chapter 8 - Stretching Your Dollars

Try to be frugal but not cheap.[1] It is frugal to eat at home or not order a soft drink at a restaurant, but it is cheap not to tip a server adequately. It is frugal to save money, but it is cheap not to provide enough for your family.

What are some ways to save money?

Not all of the following suggestions will apply to you, but some will. Some of these ideas have the potential of saving many dollars, while others can only save pennies. However, by totaling the money saved from these suggestions, the sum can go a long way toward helping you reach your savings goals.

Food [2, 3, 4, 5, 6]

1. Don't go shopping when hungry.

2. Plan menus to reduce the number of trips to the store.

3. Use menus to prepare shopping lists and buy only what is on the list.

4. Don't take others along who love junk food.

5. Do cost comparisons and understand unit pricing. (Take a calculator along.) Purchase food at lower priced food stores rather than convenience stores or vending machines.

6. Take advantage of sales. In order to recognize a good buy, you must be familiar with the regular price of items. It is a good idea to take a notepad to record the prices of items you regularly use.

7. Buy non-perishable items that are on sale in quantity, provided that you have adequate storage space. However, if it costs you more money in travel expenses than you save on your purchase, it isn't worth it.

8. Take advantage of coupon offers on items you regularly buy.

9. Buy house brands.

10. Stay away from expensive pre-prepared food, such as TV and microwave dinners and baby food. Even pre-sliced meats and cheeses are more expensive than unsliced.

11. For snacks, eat carrots, celery and fresh fruit. They are healthier than junk foods anyway.

12. Eat less meat.

13. On weekends, make big batches of chili, lasagna, soup, etc. to heat up for meals during the next week.

14. Buy from bakery thrift outlets or buy "day-old" bread.

15. Eat at restaurants only for special treats. When you do go out to eat, perhaps it could be for lunch when the prices are lower. Otherwise look for "early-bird" specials or two-for-one dining coupons. Also consider "all you can eat" buffets.

16. Drink water at restaurants rather than soft drinks or coffee.

17. Don't throw out leftovers.

Utilities[7, 8, 9]

1. Use small appliances for cooking; for example, use a toaster rather than oven.

2. Bake several items together.

3. Turn off your oven just before cooking is finished.

4. Don't open the oven door to peek in when something is cooking.

5. In winter, after using your oven turn it off and leave the door open to warm the kitchen, unless you have small children who could be burned.

6. Frequently change the bag in your vacuum cleaner and the filter on your furnace and clean the air filter on your dryer.

7. Avoid over-drying your clothes.

8. Do several dryer loads in quick sequence.

9. Get a clothesline to dry some clothes.

10. Turn off the radio and stereo when not listening.

11. Set water-heater thermostat lower.

12. Insulate your water heater.

13. Use a broom, not a hose, to clean driveways and sidewalks.

14. Repair leaky faucets.

15. Don't let the water run while brushing your teeth.

16. Take showers instead of baths.

17. Turn off lights when no one is in the room.

18. Use lower wattage bulbs in closets and halls.

19. Use automatic timers for lights when away from home.

20. Adjust the level of your washing machine for partial loads, or wait until you have a full load.

21. Use a shorter washing cycle or wash some things by hand.

22. Make sure insulation in your house is adequate.

23. Install storm windows. If you can't afford them, tape clear or translucent plastic film to the inside of your window frames.

24. Check weather stripping around doors.

25. Close the damper in the fireplace.

26. Check the ducts you can reach for air leaks.

27. Shut off heat and air conditioning in vacant parts of house.

28. Lower thermostat to 68°F in winter, and raise air conditioning to 75°F in summer. It is claimed that you raise operating costs 5% every time you up the thermostat two degrees in the winter. Rely more on wearing warm clothing in winter and light clothing in summer.

29. Use ceiling fans.

30. Put reflective film or screens on windows that get direct sunlight in the summer.

31. Let the dishes air dry.

32. Make sure that any new appliances that you purchase are energy efficient.

Telephone[10, 11, 12]

1. Dial direct rather than using an operator.

2. Place calls on weekends or at night when the rates are lower.

3. Select a long-distance carrier that has an economical pricing plan that fits your calling patterns.

4. Plan your call by making an outline ahead of time.

5. Time your calls and limit yourself. Use a timer if necessary.

6. Write letters. Many people will appreciate getting some personal mail rather than "junk" mail and bills.

7. Fax or e-mail.

Clothes[13, 14]

1. Buy clothes on sale. At certain times of the year, such as after Christmas or at the end of a season, you can expect the stores to have sales. Again, it pays to know the regular price of an item. Some stores will raise the original price (phony mark-up) and then offer a big discount to appear to be giving

a bargain. Also, some stores bring in a poor quality of clothes especially for the sale. The cheapest price is not necessarily the best buy. An item can be costly in the long run, if it doesn't last or if you don't wear it for some reason, such as a poor fit.

2. Buy clothes that will stay in style for a long time, such as a navy blue blazer for men.

3. Buy permanent press, wrinkle-free clothing.

4. Trade children's clothes among friends.

5. Shop at second-hand stores.

6. Visit garage sales.

Transportation[15, 16, 17]

1. Ride a bike or walk.

2. Consider using public transportation such as the bus.

3. Ride with someone else and share the costs.

4. Drive an economy car.

5. Inflate your tires at a higher pressure.

6. Slow down.

7. Reduce air drag by closing car windows and avoiding roof top carriers.

8. Avoid rush hour traffic if possible. If you are going to be stopped for a while during the summer, turn off your engine and roll down the windows.

9. Purchase oil and air filters at discount stores and change them yourself.

10. Buy the lowest octane gasoline that doesn't knock in your engine.

11. Do preventive maintenance, such as oil changes, to prevent costly repairs and keep your engine in tune.

12. Consider a used car.

13. Keep your car until it is worn out. In some states your licensing fees are based on the value of the car.

14. If you have to borrow, shop around for the lowest interest rate.

15. Sell your old car by advertising in the newspaper. (See precautions mentioned in Chapter 10).

16. When buying a car, decide exactly what you want and shop for the best deal.

17. Plan errands to accomplish several things in the same trip in order to save time and gasoline.

18. Eliminate collision insurance on older cars or raise the deductibles. Also, ask about applicable discounts for good students, good driving, anti-theft devices, and air bags.

19. Purchase airplane tickets 21 days in advance and watch for airfare wars. Usually, the best fares require a Saturday night stay over.

20. Shop the Internet for low fares.

21. Utilize frequent flier miles.

22. Be a courier where a company pays most of the fare to get you to deliver a package.

23. Volunteer to get bumped if the flight is overbooked. Usually they will offer hundreds of dollars, or a free ticket, if you are willing to take the next flight.

24. Shop around for the best car rental rates and avoid duplicating insurance coverage that you may already have.

Household[18, 19, 20]

1. Raise the deductibles on your homeowner's or tenant's insurance.

2. Buy slightly damaged furniture.

3. Buy used furniture.

4. Do your own repairs. Manuals are available to assist you.

Recreation

1. Exchange baby-sitting with friends.

2. Look for inexpensive forms of entertainment. Some sports, such as tennis, cost very little.

3. Take a camping vacation using a tent or trailer.

Gifts

1. Agree with brothers and sisters not to exchange gifts.

2. For most relatives, just send cards or a newsletter, while for others set a reasonable limit and stick with it.

3. Take advantage of after-Christmas sales to buy Christmas wrapping and cards.

Funeral[21, 22]

1. Make your wishes known about your funeral or burial arrangements in writing.

2. Call or visit several funeral homes and ask for prices and services.

Miscellaneous[23, 24, 25]

1. Recycle aluminum cans.

2. Squeeze slivers of soap onto new bars.

3. Rent items that you don't often use.

4. Swap services, time and tools with neighbors.

5. Reduce your life insurance when your children are grown, and you have less financial responsibilities.

6. Select a bank that offers free checking and pays interest.

7. Ask physicians and pharmacists for generic drugs whenever appropriate.

8. If you are a senior, ask for senior discounts.

What other sources of information are available regarding how to save money?

1. Discuss with friends how they save money.

2. Subscribe to money-saving newsletters.

   A. Frugal Family Network Newsletter. You can subscribe to this newsletter by sending a check for $10.00 per year to Frugal Family Network, PO Box 92731, Austin, TX 78709. They offer a money-back guarantee if you don't save money. Also, at no cost, you can find some ways to save money on their web site www.frugalfamilynetwork.com.

   B. The Dollar Stretcher has weekly articles that provide tips on saving money and improving your life. Their web site www.stretcher.com contains several articles describing money saving ideas.

   C. The Cheapskate Monthly can be subscribed to either by mail or online at their web site www.cheapskatemonthly.com. Also online, at no cost, is the tip of the day, as well as many reader-submitted tips. You can purchase a book from them entitled *Tiptionary* by Mary Hunt, which contains more than 2300 tips for saving money, time, and energy for $7.19.

   D. Skinflint Newsletter, Tightwad Living, PO Box 629, Burgin, KY, 40310. By writing this address and sending a self-addressed, stamped envelope, you may obtain a sample of Melodie Moore's monthly newsletter. Also, you can obtain a 150-page book of money saving tips, recipes, and formulas for $7.99, postage included.

   E. Creative Downscaling. This newsletter has six issues per year and can be ordered from Creative Downscaling,

P.O. Box 1884, Jonesboro, GA, 30237-1884 for $15.00 per year. Their web site www.mindspring.com~kilgo/index did not have much to offer at the time of this writing.

F. The Pocket Change Investor. For $12.95 per year you can order this quarterly newsletter from Good Advice Press, P.O. Box 78, Elizaville, NY, 12523. Their web site www.goodadvicepress.com has excellent advice on many areas of personal finance.

G. The Frugal Gazette. This twelve-page newsletter comes out every month and costs $12.00 per year. It can be ordered from The Frugal Gazette, P.O. Box 3395, Newtown, Connecticut, 06470-3395. To receive a free copy of The Frugal Gazette send a business size self-addressed stamped envelope (SASE) to the above address. Their web site www.frugalgazette.com contains sample newsletter articles.

Should a Person Shop on the Internet?

I personally think this is the wave of the future. Companies can market on the Internet without having to maintain expensive display rooms and sales personnel. I recently purchased a CPAP device (breathing machine for sleep apnea) for less than half of what it would have cost me if I would have purchased it from local suppliers. You can even buy automobiles on the Internet, as described in Chapter 10.

---

[1] Burkett, *The Complete Financial Guide for Young Couples*, 15

[2] Galloway, 133-134.

[3] Burkett, *Answers To Your Family's Financial Questions*, 61.

[4] Moffett, Martha, *How to Get Out of Debt – and Save Enough Money to Enjoy the Sweet Life*, MicroMags, 600 S.E. Coast Avenue, Lantana, FL, 1996, 53-60.

[5] MacGregor, 72-80.

[6] 66 Ways To Save Money, Save Money, Consumer Federation of America, 1424 16th Street NW, Suite 604, Washington, DC.

[7] Galloway, 137.

[8] Moffett, 44-50.

[9] 66 Ways to Save Money.

[10] Galloway, 135.

[11] 66 Ways to Save Money.

[12] Moffett, 37.

[13] Galloway, 135-136.

[14] Moffett, 67.

[15] Galloway, 136-137.

[16] Moffett, 39, 82-88.

[17] 66 Ways to Save Money.

[18] Moffett, 35, 50-51.

[19] Anderson, 70.

[20] How to Manage Your Financial Resources, 10.

[21] 66 Ways to Save Money.

[22] Anderson, 73-74.

[23] Moffett, 25, 65.

[24] How to Manage Your Financial Resources, 10.

[25] 66 Ways to Save Money.

Chapter 9 - Developing Sales Resistance

How can a person control impulse spending?

1. Don't buy anything not budgeted unless you wait at least thirty days. Use this time away from sales pressure to "count the cost." Counsel with other people, especially your spouse. "It's not in my budget" is what you can reply to those pressuring you to buy.

2. Get at least three prices for the same item from different sources.

3. Create an "impulse list." An impulse list can only have one thing on it at a time, and you must wait 30 days after putting it on the list to purchase it. If, during the 30 days, you find something else you like better, then cross out the original item and write down the new item (with the date). After 30 days you may purchase this item if you can afford it.[1]

4. Recognize that greed is often the motivation for impulse buying. You feel you have to have more and you have to have the best. The "I-owe-it-to-myself" philosophy must be overcome by God's word. Perhaps God wants you to live in an apartment complex so you can witness there. You should ask, "What is God's plan for me?"[2]

What questions should be asked before buying something?

1. Do I really need it? Nothing is a bargain if you don't need it.[3]

2. Can I afford it? If buying is going to make you spend more than you make, you cannot afford the purchase.

3. Do I need something else more?

4. Can I get along well without it?[4]

5. Is it a current model? Last year's model car may have depreciated far more than what you save.[5]

6. Is this the best time to buy? Will this item be on sale soon?[6]

7. If the item is on sale, is it a true sale price?[7] Some suitcases we looked at were supposedly 1/3 off, but we found the same model at another store where the regular price was less than sale price at the first store.

8. Can I substitute something else for this? Just plain walking may be as good or better than some expensive exercise equipment.[8]

9. Have I checked and researched the item? Magazines, such as Consumer Reports, evaluate various products for performance, value, and maintenance reports. You can usually find these at a local library without having to subscribe to the magazine.[9]

10. Do I know the retailer's reputation? Do they replace unsatisfactory products? Have they been in business for a long time? Do the products have a warranty?[10]

11. Will this item contribute to our family unity?

12. Is this item expensive to maintain?

13. Does it complement my Christian testimony?

If your answer is negative to any of the questions, except number three, four, eight, and twelve, you probably are not being a good steward of the Lord's money.

What are some techniques that Overspender's Anonymous recommends?

Jeanne Fioretto founded a group called Overspender's Anonymous (O$A) where people with the same problem help one another. It is to overspenders what Weight Watchers is to the overweight and Alcoholics Anonymous is to the alcoholic. There are many different reasons why people are overspenders, but a "common thread" seems to be the search for something that will make them feel better or maintain their self-esteem. Sometimes overspending is an attempt to buy substitutes for the affection, intimacy or sense of accomplishment the person needs. Some think the change that they desire will be accomplished with a new look in clothes or by redecorating their home. Others, who are unhappy at work or at home, tend to console themselves with expensive adult toys, such as elaborate sound systems, and boats. O$A has a support network which includes a telephone team that can be called when someone is having trouble resisting the sales, shopping buddies who can go along when someone shops, and group meetings where dubious purchases can be discussed. In a group you realize that others behave the same way. If you can identify the problem, accept the responsibility, want to change, and if necessary get help, you can overcome spending problems.[11]

---

[1] Burkett, *The Complete Financial Guide for Young Couples*, 36.

[2] Ibid., 47.

[3] MacGregor, 64, 65.

[4] Galloway, 82.

[5] MacGregor, 65.

[6] Ibid., 65.

[7] Ibid., 66.

[8] Ibid., 67.

[9] Ibid., 69.

[10] Ibid., 69.

[11] Rodgers, Mary Augusta, "How I Cut My Crazy Spending," Woman's Day, September 23, 1980.

Chapter 10 - Buying A Car

In our society transportation is usually a need and not a luxury. This need may decrease in the future when more people are allowed to work at home via the computer, but, for the present, a person usually needs to get back and forth from work in order to hold a job.

Since automobiles are very expensive to operate what other alternatives for transportation should be considered?

1. Is it possible that you could walk back and forth to work? If time, distance and weather permit, you could save a lot of money and get a lot of exercise.

2. How about riding a bike? This would be much faster than walking and would also save a lot of money.

3. Is public transportation available? Bus and subway fares are usually less expensive than operating a car. Also, if you work in a city, taking a bus would save you parking fees, and, while you are riding, you can use the time reading. You should not try reading while you are driving!

4. Could you ride with someone else and pay for the rides? He or she might be delighted to have someone assist with the expenses. In some cities there are special carpool lanes which are faster than the single occupant car lanes. Also, some places waive the toll for crossing bridges to vehicles with 2 or more people during rush hours. These are incentives to reduce traffic and air pollution.

In considering the above alternatives one must ask if it is safe to walk, ride a bike, or take public transportation. In some areas a car may be a safer option. In ride sharing, a person must be flexible in case the driver has to work overtime or has other schedule changes.

What area of your budget has the biggest potential for cost cutting?

Transportation is probably the area of your budget where you can make the most significant savings. Remember a dollar saved is a dollar earned, while a dollar earned is not a dollar saved due to taxes and tithes.

The cost to operate an automobile includes gasoline, depreciation, insurance, annual motor vehicle fees, tires, oil and repairs. In 1998 the IRS standard mileage deduction for operating an automobile was 32.5 cents a mile. A new car actually costs much more to operate than this according to rental car companies and the tables below.[1]

Age of Car when purchased (years old)	Average Cost per mile
0	$.49
1 year old	.38
2	.35
3	.34
4	.34
5	.34
6	.33
7	.33
8	.33
9	.33

The longer a car is driven, the cheaper it becomes to own. The cheapest car you can ever own is usually the car you presently own. Continuing to drive your old car may be the best way you can decrease your living expenses.[2] Avoid car payments if at all possible. The automobile is one item that keeps many families in hot water financially. Costs of repairs are usually minor compared to monthly payments

Should a person buy a used car or a new one?

Why do Americans spend over $300 billion on 35 million used cars each year when quality used cars are difficult to find, hard to evaluate, and carry the worst reputation of any product on the market? The answer to this is that they cost on the average $10,000 less than a new car and cost less to operate. Also, there are emotional benefits. For example, a new scrape or noise is not as bothersome on a used car as it is on a new one.[3] Car dealers now prefer to advertise used cars as "pre-owned" cars to improve their image.

How do the operating costs of a used car differ from those of a new car?

1. **Less**

   A. **Depreciation.** This is the amount the car drops in value with time. Without question, depreciation is the biggest expense on a new car, unless the car is driven many more miles than normal. The depreciation of a new car during the first year will probably be 20% to 30% of the original price; therefore, the newer the car, the greater the depreciation.[4]

   B. **Insurance.** On an older car you can usually afford the risk of losses incurred to your automobile and thus can drop the collision portion of your insurance. You must always carry liability insurance. If you can't afford liability insurance you can't afford to drive.

   C. **License fees.** In many states the annual cost of the license fee is determined by the estimated value of the vehicle.

2. **Same**

   A. **Tires.** The cost for tires will vary with the size and type of tires and your driving habits, but will usually be less than $.01/mile. These costs will be higher if your wheels are out of alignment.

B. **Gasoline.** Depending on the miles per gallon the car gets and the price per gallon, the cost of gasoline will usually range between $.05 to $.14/mile.

C. **Oil changes and filters.** This will usually cost less than $.01/mile.

3. **More**

A. **Repairs.** Repair expenses usually increase when the car has more mileage and gets older. It is very difficult to estimate this. If these costs exceed $.10/mile you are probably ready to get a different car.

B. **Oil.** New cars usually use little or no oil except for oil changes, while an older car may use more oil. If this costs more than $.01/mile you will probably get a ticket for polluting the air.

Due to the lower cost of operating a used car, almost every financial advisor will recommend purchasing a good used car rather than a new one. A two to three-year-old car will have depreciated considerably but will still have some time remaining on the factory warranty. Some cars have as much as a seven-year warranty on the drive train. There are some situations, however, that I feel warrant purchasing a new car, if you are financially able. Some jobs, such as those involved in real estate, may encourage having a new car to promote a successful image. You might also need the latest features, such as dual air bags or antilock brakes. Also, if you intend to keep a car for a long period of time, or you drive a lot of miles, the average depreciation per year is greatly reduced. If you are the original owner, you know how the car has been treated and maintained, and you know the condition of the car. A new car will probably have at least a 3-year 36,000-mile warranty. So repair costs, except for accidents, should be almost non-existent for the first three years. So if you cannot be without a car due to a mechanical breakdown, a new car may be a wise choice.

What kind of vehicle should a person buy?

First, you should figure out what kind of vehicle suits your lifestyle and budget. There are subcompact, compact, mid-size and full-size cars. There are premium and sports coupes and premium sedans. Also, there are sport-utility vehicles and minivans. You have to determine your needs. If you want to haul a lot of people, then you must have a minivan or van. If you will be going off-road a lot, then consider a sport-utility vehicle or a truck. On the other hand, if economy is a factor, then consider a subcompact or compact. If safety is a prime concern, then you would want a larger vehicle. You might also need to find out what the insurance premiums will be. Some vehicles have better safety records and thus lower rates. If you are married, you should discuss this thoroughly with your spouse. Next, consider cars that have held up well in the past on the basis of frequency of repair reports. *Consumer Reports* gives a list of reliable used cars in various price ranges and a list of cars to avoid. They rate cars based on frequency of repairs for the following trouble spots: engine, cooling, fuel, ignition, transmission, clutch, electrical, air-conditioning, suspension, brakes, exhaust, body rust, paint/trim, integrity, and hardware.[5, 6] Edmund's ratings are presented in graphical and numerical form on a 1 to 10 scale, 10 being the best in the categories of safety, reliability, performance, comfort, driving enjoyment, and value.[7]

What are some sources for a used car?

1. **New car dealers** are usually the most trustworthy sources for late-model used cars.[8] They often keep only the best trade-ins for resale. While new car dealers often charge a higher price, they often will provide a warranty for some period of time. If possible, buy from a dealer of the same brand because they are likely to have cheaper parts and may make the repairs. With a new car dealer, there is a better chance the car has been inspected.[9] Cars that don't meet the dealer's criteria are auctioned off.

2. **Used car dealers** often get castoffs from auctions or new car dealers. While they often sell at a lower price than the new car dealer does, the cars are often sold "as is." If you do buy from a used car dealer, buy from one who has been around a long time.[10, 11]

3. **Auto-rental agencies** such as Hertz, Avis and National offer some cars to the public. Some companies provide limited warranties. They often have a good selection of domestic and imported models. They usually keep maintenance records and sell late models, 12 to 18 months old with high mileage. However, you don't negotiate the price, and the cars are often loaded with options you may not want.[12]

4. **Private owners** usually offer the lowest price because the overhead of car dealers and sales commission do not have to be paid. However, with this method you receive no warranty, it requires a lot of running around, and it is very time consuming. Most used cars are purchased directly from a private party. About half are between friends and acquaintances.[13] If you are buying from someone you know, you may get honest information about the car. You should ask whether the seller is a dealer. Some unethical dealers pose as ordinary citizens to sell their cars.[14]

5. **Auctions** usually sell cars that have been rejected; therefore, I don't recommend this as a source for used cars unless you are a mechanic.

What questions can be asked on the telephone to save time when buying a used car from a newspaper advertisement?[15, 16]

When buying a used car from a newspaper advertisement you can usually determine from the ad the make, model, engine size and features of the car, such as automatic transmission, air conditioning, color, power steering, power brakes, power windows, and whether it has an AM/FM radio and tape player. You might ask the condition of these items and ask the following questions.

1. How long have you owned the car?

2. Did you buy the car new?

3. What is the mileage?

4. Has the car generally been driven around town or on long trips?

5. Was this the only car in your family?

6. What do you like best about the car?

7. What major repair work has been done on the car?

8. Has the car ever been wrecked?

9. Have you ever had any problems with rust? Has the car ever been painted?

10. Why are you selling the car?

11. Did you follow the manufacturer's recommended maintenance schedule?

12. Has the car ever been recalled?

13. Where do you generally get your service performed?

14. What would be needed to get the car into top shape?

15. Are there any liens on the car?

How can the value of a used car be determined?

The following are two of the best sources for determining used car values are:

1. **The Blue Book.** Actually there are two books sometimes referred to as the blue book. The *Kelley Blue Book* and the *N.A.D.A. (National Automobile Dealers Association) Official Used Car Guide*, which is actually orange and is published in nine separate regional editions which show the average trade-in or wholesale price, the average loan price, and the average retail price. Mileage table adjustments, as well as adjustments for various options, are included. These books

are available at most libraries,[17] and the Kelley Blue Book can be found on the internet at www.kbb.com/pubs.html

2. ***Edmund's Used Car Prices and Ratings*** is published quarterly. As far as I know there are no regional versions, but this book gives information similar to the "blue book." In addition, it rates the cars based on performance, comfort, driving pleasure, value, and overall rating. Edmund's includes a short description of model updates for the model year. It also includes the recall data since 1984. When pricing a specific vehicle you must take into account its condition. Edmund's pricing is assuming the car is "clean" (fine physical and mechanical condition). A vehicle in superb condition known as a "cream puff" will command a higher price, while a car in worse condition will have less value. For a "rough" vehicle (one needing repairs) the cost of repairs should be subtracted from the value of a clean car of the same make and model year.[18] In reality, what a particular car is worth is what someone is willing to pay for it.[19] These books are available at many grocery stores, bookstores and also on the Internet at www.edmunds.com.

How can a person check out a used car?

Hunting for a used car is very time consuming. You may wish to go alone at first. When you do find a car you like, test drive it and observe its general condition inside and out. If you think you might want to buy it, do not negotiate at this time but write down the make, model, year, mileage, and exact options. Come back at another time, bringing along your spouse or a friend, to do a more thorough job of inspecting the vehicle. It is easier to inspect a car if you bring a friend along to help. Don't purchase a used car in the rain or when wet because the water hides the defects in the paint. *Consumer Reports Buying Guide* gives a number of things to look for regarding fluids, body integrity, tires, suspension, and interior. It also tells how to check during the road test for steering, engine, transmission, brakes, comfort, and quietness.[20] *Jack Gillis' Guide to Best and Worst*

Used Cars includes extensive checklists for the inside, outside, under the hood, odometer, and safety. He also gives pointers regarding the test drive and a mechanics checklist.[21]

After the inspection and test-drive, discuss all aspects of the car with your spouse or friend. A car that meets your approval is ready for checking by a reliable mechanic or auto diagnostic center. Unless a dealer lets you get a pre-purchase inspection, don't buy a used car from him without some kind of free or low-priced bumper-to-bumper warranty. If you're buying from a private party, make sure you have your mechanic check the car thoroughly before you buy it. Get a written estimate of needed repairs to use in price negotiations.[22]

Why does a dealer often make more money on a used car than a new one?

If you are buying a used car from a car dealer, keep in mind that many dealers make more money on a used car than a new one because it is easier for a consumer to find out the exact dealer cost on a new car. On a used car you don't know what the dealer paid for the car or allowed for it on a trade-in. It's not unusual for a dealer to make $2,000 to $3,000 profit on a used car selling for $10,000, so there is plenty of room to negotiate.

How does a person negotiate a price?

With the help of the above price guides, plus comparison shopping, you must determine, to the best of your ability, what the car is worth before you negotiate to buy it. To get the best deal on a car you will probably have to terminate negotiations and walk out at least once before you get what you want.[23] You will probably have to use some of the same tactics that are described later in "How does a person negotiate the best deal on a new car." Don't fall for the line that the price a salesman quoted is only good for that day. If the car is clean and your timing is right, you can probably start negotiating at a price $500 below the wholesale value. That is probably what he obtained it for in a trade. If the car had needed expensive repairs, he probably would have wholesaled it. Probably the person selling the car will not accept this offer and will make a counter offer. If you still want the car, increase your offer in increments. I question whether you are getting a good buy if you pay more than $500 above the wholesale value.

What should a person do before buying a new car?

A good suggestion is to invest in a paperback book such as *Consumer Guide-Rating The New Autos*. This book tells which autos are in each category, such as sub-compact, compact, etc. Most of the book has the cars arranged alphabetically by manufacturer. Two pages are provided for each automobile. These pages include a picture of the auto, a brief description of its features and options, warranties, specifications, and ratings according to performance, accommodations, workmanship, and value. Later in the book, the retail price, dealer invoice, and fair price are shown for each model and option.[24] By studying this book you should be able to narrow your choices without even going to a dealer. Certainly the book gives an indication whether a certain car will fit in your budget. Remember that, in addition to the price of the car, you will have to pay sales tax and license fees. You should allow approximately 10% of the price of the car for these costs. If you can only afford to spend $10,000, then forget about a Lexus or a Mercedes Benz as a new car. It may serve you better to go back to the section on buying a used car, or else keep your present car until you can save some more.

You should consider not only the initial cost of the car but also the predicted reliability based on the records of previous cars of this model and manufacturer. Maintenance costs are higher with some types of cars. In addition, consider the expected residual value of the car. This is the expected future value. Banks and leasing companies do much research in order to anticipate what a car will be worth at the end of the lease. This figure is used in the calculations to determine lease payments. For your purposes, the residual value is the value this car will have when you trade it in. Thus, what the car costs you while you own it will be the cost (price, insurance, license fees, tires, repairs, gasoline and oil) minus what you get when you sell it or trade it in.[25]

What should you accomplish on your first visit to a car dealer?

The purpose of your first visit to the car dealer is not to negotiate a price, but to obtain information about models that you might possibly purchase. Let the salesperson know that you are a serious buyer but that you won't be making a deal for a few days. Have the sales person demonstrate the various features of the car and take a test drive. Take notes on the positive and negative features and write down the retail price of the car and its factory installed options. Ask them for literature on the model, an accessory menu that lists all of the dealer installed accessories available, and the retail price for each. Ask about their service department hours, labor-rates; whether they provide loaners and a shuttle service; and whether they would have any problem servicing a car that you have purchased from some other dealer. Ask them why you should do business with them rather than with one of their competitors. Find out if there are currently any factory rebates or interest incentives. If so, look at the written guidelines for the incentive. Talk to as many dealers as possible until you are confident that you have enough information to decide on a specific car and a specific dealer.[26]

What does a dealer pay for a car?

Most new car buyers pay thousands of dollars more for a car than they have to because they don't know how much the dealer pays for a car. You can find the dealer invoice price in books such as *Edmund's New Car Prices*[27] or *Consumer Guide*.[28] The "dealer invoice" is the price that the dealer actually pays to buy the new car from the manufacturer. His real cost, though, may end up being lower than the invoice amount if he is eligible for dealer holdback. Dealer holdback is a specific percentage or dollar amount that the manufacturer holds back from a dealer until a car is sold. This holdback is pure profit for the dealer since he doesn't have to share it with the salesmen. This holdback is usually 2% to 3% of the Manufacturer's Suggested Retail Price (MSRP), which is attached to the window of the car. In addition, some models carry Factory-to-Dealer cash incentives, which are designed to increase sales of slow-moving cars. Also, when the new models come out, dealers often receive a credit for 5% of the MSRP on every unsold new vehicle that just became "last year's model." From the above information, you can see that you can buy a car below the invoice price, and the dealer can still make money from dealer holdbacks and various incentives.

The factory-to-dealer incentives discussed above are different from customer incentives commonly called "customer rebates." Customer rebates always belong to the buyer and are not negotiable. These rebates can be applied to either the down payment, if the car is financed, or to the purchase price, if the car is being purchased with cash.

While a person will have to pay a destination charge, one should never have to pay advertising or floor plan charges (interest costs incurred by the dealer for financing the new cars on his lot). These charges are just normal expenses that a dealer has to pay for doing business.[29] It is claimed that 95% of all cars sold in the United States with a MSRP less than $30,000 can be purchased somewhere between dealer invoice and $500 over invoice.[30] There are, however, some models of cars and trucks that are in great demand. You will not be able to purchase these models for only $500 over invoice.

Why is the "best price" on a car not always the best deal?

Car buyers often shop for the best price on the basic car and then are allowed a lower trade-in value on their old car or are outmaneuvered into paying a higher price for options and finance charges in the finance and insurance office. Also, they often get sold things, like rust-proofing, paint sealant, fabric protection and extended warranties, that they don't need.[31, 32] The car that you buy should have all options installed at the factory, rather than at the dealer, to obtain the best possible negotiating edge. If you have to finance a car you will probably get a better rate through your bank or credit union. You would probably do best to find out what interest rates you can get from your own source before you reach the finance and insurance manager of the car dealer. A small increase in interest rates can cause a huge difference in what you pay in total for a car. For example, for each percentage point the interest increases on a 60-month, $10,000 loan, you will pay more than $250. Dealers make a great deal of money through the financing office.[33]

Never ask a salesman what his best price is, because he probably doesn't know what the sales manager will accept on a given day. And even if he did know, he wouldn't give it to you, because you would take the price to another dealer to negotiate an even lower price. If he does give you a price it probably will be a lowball price which won't be accepted when you actually make the offer. "Lowballing" is basically an outright lie, quoting someone a low price to get them to come in, and then making up an excuse as to why they can't sell the car at that price. A price a salesman gives you is worthless.[34]

How are car salespersons paid?

What most people don't realize is that the salesperson gets paid approximately 25-30 % of the gross profit made on the deal. Thus, the more he can charge you the more money he makes.[35] Car dealers consistently make more profit with women buyers than with men. Once the woman buyer is convinced that the salesman (we will assume he is male since less than 5% of sales persons in the auto industry are female) is sincere and ethical, she becomes much more at ease and trusting than the average male buyer.[36]

What is the "bait and switch" technique?

In general, the American car buyer is simply no match for the shrewd, educated, and cunning car dealer.[37] One technique they use is called "bait and switch." In this scam, the newspaper advertisement describes a great car at a low price, but when you go to the dealer they will show you a different car than the advertised car, or they will tell you it was just sold. Then they try to sell you another car at a different price.[38]

When is the best time to buy a new car?

Timing is very important in negotiating a good deal on a car. The right time to buy a car is when you are fully prepared to outmaneuver the most cunning salesperson.[39] However, the calendar is also of the utmost importance. The right timing can save you hundreds of dollars. Many times car dealers will lose incentive money or allocations of the most desirable models if they do not reach certain volumes. Dealers then pressure their sales managers, who in turn pressure the salesmen, to meet monthly objectives. The pressure exerted on salesmen in the last five days of the month is at its peak. Salesmen and sales managers can earn substantial month-end bonuses if they meet their particular goals. As a result, the best time to buy a car is usually at the end of the month. They might give you a good price and everybody wins. You get a good price and they get a nice bonus. This occurs only if you take actual delivery of the car before the end of the month.[40] You might also consider shopping when few buyers are around. Go on a weekday, when the weather is bad, and around holidays like Christmas or during the Super Bowl.[41]

How does a person negotiate the best deal on a new car?

After you have obtained all the information necessary to select the car you want, you are ready to visit the car dealer to negotiate. Call the dealership to set up an appointment to buy a new car. You have determined beforehand exactly the model and features that you want and the actual cash difference that you are willing to pay for the car. Ask to test drive the model that you want to buy once more to be certain that you have made the right choice. Do not allow them to talk you into accepting fewer features or to focus your attention on monthly payments rather than a cash difference. Keep in mind that a car dealer will not accept any deal until he is certain that he has squeezed every penny out of your pocket. Expect to play the back and forth game with the salesman and sales manager. Be prepared to devote at least an hour strictly to the negotiating process.[42]

Make certain that the model you are buying has a manufacturer's suggested retail price that matches the price disclosed in your buyer's guide, including all factory-installed options and destination charges. Make sure the salesman writes the correct prices for the car and options on the buyer's order. Initially offer the salesman $500 below the dealer invoice price minus the actual cash value of the trade-in, minus any factory incentives. If you have a trade-in, the salesman will get it appraised at this time and will bring the appraisal on your car and your signed offer to the sales manager.[43]

You can almost be certain that your initial offer will be rejected, so offer an additional $200 and insist that he take your counter offer to the sales manager. If this offer is not accepted by the sales manager, offer him an additional $150. If he returns again with bad news, tell the salesman you need some time to think about it and get up from his office and take a little walk to give them time to sweat a while. Come back with one more offer of an additional $150 saying, "If the sales manager won't accept this offer please return my keys and I will leave." More than likely the salesman will return, not with your keys, but rather with a closer or the sales manager. The salesman realizes that he is going to lose the sale on his terms so he "turns over" the buyer to the "closer." Whoever returns with the salesman will be a seasoned professional who specializes in extracting money from customers who insist that they won't pay one penny more. The "closer" comes in rested and with a clear head ready to start all over again. Insist that you plan on visiting other dealers (naming some specifically), but to save time you could offer $100 more. Tell the salesman or closer to take another look at your trade-in. If they accept, you have negotiated a deal for $100 above dealer cost. If they don't accept, tell them you are going to check their competition, but if they change their minds they should call you. Then, actually leave the dealership. A dealer will not let you leave only a few dollars away from a deal.[44]

When you have made a deal, check the retail price, the cash difference, license fees, etc. on the paper work. When the salesman is finished he will turn you over to the finance and insurance manager as mentioned before.[45]

What do the four squares represent in the structured method of selling?

Salesmen often use a structured selling system to control and confuse you. One method is called the four-square system, in which the salesman takes a piece of paper and draws two lines (one vertical and one horizontal) dividing the paper into four squares. The squares represent selling price, trade allowance, down payment and monthly payment.[46] They can confuse an ordinary buyer by writing down a high trade-in but using the manufacturer's suggested retail price as the price. No one should pay this for an automobile. Also, they can write down a low down payment and low monthly payments by extending the number of months that you pay. Do not get suckered into the monthly payment trap. Your first negotiation should be strictly on the price of the actual car with your desired options. The value of your trade-in is also negotiable just like the price you pay for the car. You should determine the approximate value of your car before negotiating your present car as a trade-in. Don't expect to get more than the wholesale value of your trade-in. If you do, you probably have not negotiated well the price for the new car. There are different automobile terms that relate to the value of a used car - actual cash value (ACV) and gross trade-allowance (GTA). For example, let's say you are purchasing a new car with a factory sticker price of $16,000, and they allow you $7,000 for your trade-in making the difference of what you owe $9,000. You may think that the $7,000 they allowed was great. However, if you had negotiated properly you might have purchased the new car for $14,000. Thus, while the GTA was $7,000, in actuality, they only allowed you $5,000 (ACV).[47]

Should I trade in my old car or sell it outright?

Usually you will obtain more for your car if you sell it outright through the newspapers. Car dealers will usually buy a car for the wholesale value deducting about three times what they think it will cost them to prepare the vehicle for resale. Rarely will they buy a car for more than the $500 under the wholesale value. However, to sell a car by yourself requires some time and skill. You need to ask some questions: If you sell your car, will it cause a transportation problem for your family? Will the sale force you to buy another car in a hurry and perhaps make a big mistake? How much do you value your time? How much will it cost to advertise the car? Are you prepared to accept the phone calls and set up appointments for people to drive and inspect your car?[48] Do you like negotiating the price? Are you afraid for your safety with strangers?[49] If you sell the car by yourself ask for a certified check or cash for the car.[50]

On the other hand, your trade-in can be an important tool during the negotiating process with a dealer. At the end of the month he may stretch the appraisal on a used car just to make a deal on a new car. Before you bring in a car for a trade-in, spend some time and money making your car shine. Car appraisers will be influenced by a car that has been cleaned inside and out. Empty and vacuum the trunk and try to give the car a fresh smell.[51]

What other tactics do some salesmen use?

1. **The question.** "The question" is a tool that car salesmen use to manipulate and control buyers. These are some trick questions: "If I can get you $5,000 on your trade-in, will you buy today?" or "Will you buy today if we can get your monthly payments down to $250?" These questions are designed to cause you to make a commitment that you feel morally obligated to keep.

You can answer the questions with, "I don't know," or "I'll think it over," or else turn the conversation around by asking, "Would you sell me this car at $900 below invoice?" Remember, you are not obligated to buy a car until you've signed the contract.[52]

2. **The deposit.** The buyer is falsely told that he must attach a deposit to his offer before the sales manager will take it seriously. The buyer's deposit check is then "lost" to prevent him from leaving after his offer is turned down, giving the salesman more time to wear down his victim.[53] Most reputable dealers will not require a deposit with the offer.

3. **We can't find your keys.** This scam works just like "the deposit." The salesman asks for your car keys to have your car appraised while you're talking. The keys are temporarily "misplaced" to prevent you from leaving while they continue to work you over. Always bring an extra set of keys with you when you go shopping for a car. Leave immediately and tell the salesman to call you when they find your keys.[54] Customer satisfaction indexes are causing more dealers to insist that their salesmen not use these types of tactics.

4. **The Raise (or Bump).** After you have made an offer they will usually come back asking for more money. The salesman will return either with a ridiculously high counter offer or he will say you need to up the offer. Examples are "We're about $2,000 apart; let's split the difference," or "I'm working real hard to get this deal through for you. I think I can talk my boss into it if you can go up another $1,000."[55]

Why should a person avoid the commissioned car salesman if possible?

Every person who has ever bought a new car has probably experienced one or more of the above tricks. Most people dislike the entire "haggling" process of car buying and usually pay too much for a car. At the present time, Saturn dealers have the only true non-negotiable prices in the country. Saturn buyers pay retail (MSRP) for their car. Saturn salesmen are paid a salary instead of a commission, thus eliminating the pressure to get as much as they can from the customer. As enjoyable as this is for buyers, it's even more enjoyable for the dealers because they get retail for every Saturn they sell. Thus, removing the negotiating process from car buying is good for the dealer, but it doesn't benefit the adept buyer. You should stay away from one-price dealers if your mission is to pay as little as possible for the new car of your choice.[56]

The best way to avoid the commissioned car salesman is to go over his head. If possible, deal directly with the owner of the dealership. This is sometimes possible in small towns. The best car buying experience I have ever had was negotiating for a new Ford Explorer from Jim Satcher Ford, Johnston, South Carolina. After calling and visiting a number of Ford dealers in the Augusta, Georgia area, I called Jim Satcher Ford and Jim Satcher himself answered. I made an appointment to see him, and I dealt directly with him. I eliminated all of the back and forth process with the salesman and the sales manager. Since there was no salesman's commission involved, all that was a factor was the profit the dealer made.

If you can't deal with the owner, sometimes you can deal directly with the fleet manager or the sales manager. Try calling to make an appointment. Some will refuse, saying that is why they have salesmen.

If you have no trade-in, you might write or fax the fleet managers of a number of dealers. In your letter state that you are going to buy a specific model new vehicle, listing the color and any options. Then ask them to quote you their best price. Mention that you are also getting quotes from other dealers in your area and the one with the lowest quote gets your business. Let them know you're aware of the dealer invoice and any factory-to-dealer incentives, so you expect the most competitive bids to be far below MSRP. Be sure to mention that you do not want anything added to the car that is not factory installed. Your letter should have your name and address, both home and work phone numbers and a fax number if you have one. Close by stating that you will be making a final decision in two weeks, so you will assume the dealers who do not respond are not interested. Thank them in advance, sign your name, mail the letters, and wait for a response. If you can fax the letters, the whole process will be shortened by about a week.[57]

What about using a car buying service?

People who do not have the ability or desire to do battle with car dealers might consider using a service called CarBargains. CarBargains will make dealers compete with each other for your business. If you are able to buy a car at a price lower than the best quote included in their report, without using their report, they will gladly refund your entire fee of $150. Their address is CarBargains, 733 15th Street NW, Suite 820, Washington, D.C., 20005.

Dealers know that CarBargains will get at least five quotes. They also know that anyone who has paid the $150 fee is a serious buyer. Since the dealers know that they are competing with other dealers, they know that they have to bid low in order to obtain the business. Also, dealers know that if CarBargains does not get a good price locally they will get quotes from dealers outside the area who will deliver locally.[58]

Can you buy an automobile on the Internet?

Yes, there are such web sites. An example is www.Autobytel.com. Their slogan is "We're changing the way America buys cars." On this web site you can get the MSRP, dealer invoice, and option pricing for practically any make and model of vehicle. You can also get information regarding used cars. Once you are ready to buy, you submit the make, model, and other relevant information. They have an accredited dealer contact you after they have found the car, and they offer it to you at a low, competitive price. You go to the dealership, and if you like what you see, you buy the vehicle at the agreed-upon price. Autobytel claims that in less than three years, more than 1.5 million prospective car buyers have submitted requests.

According to the testimonials on their web site, there seems to be many people who are satisfied with this no hassling, no haggling experience in car buying.

What should a person do when they take delivery of a new car?

When the time comes for you to take delivery, carefully scrutinize every detail in the daylight. This includes the serial number, mileage and options. If the car has more than 250 miles on it, demand an explanation. Also check the body paint and see how the doors, trunk, hood, and windows open and close. Inspect the upholstery, carpet and headliner. Have the salesman demonstrate how to operate all equipment and accessories and do one more road test. When you're done with the inspection and road test, have the dealer make a copy of your "defect list." Then have them call you after they've fixed everything on the list. After this, do another quick inspection to make sure the repairs were done and that it didn't get any new dents or scratches while it was in the service department.[59] Be sure you have the warranty book and maintenance schedule.

Enjoy your new car. I hope that you will have chosen the right model at the best price, and that you will plan to keep the car for a long time.

What about leasing a car?

Since many automobile owners are holding onto their cars longer or else buying late model used cars, automakers are coming up with plans to get people to buy new cars more often. Relatively low initial costs and monthly payments make leasing look attractive. The problem occurs when you have little or no equity to show for your payments at the end of the lease. When the lease is up, the car still belongs to the leasing company.

There are two types of leases, an open-end and a closed-end lease. On an open-end lease, if the value of the car is less than the previously calculated expected residual value of the car, the person leasing must pay the difference. Very few companies still offer open-end leases because these leases leave the customer with practically no options. These types of leases were used by unscrupulous dealers and gave automotive leasing a very bad name. With a closed-end lease, the bank guarantees that the car will be worth a certain residual value if it is under the mileage requirements and has only normal wear and tear.

With closed-end leasing, you have four options when your lease is complete. The first option is to walk away from the car. If the mileage does not exceed the allotted amount, and there was normal wear and tear, you terminate the lease having no car and owing nothing. On the other hand, if you exceed the mileage allotment, or you have such things as tears in the upholstery and significant dents, then you have to pay for this at the end of the lease. The extra mileage charge is specified in the lease. Make sure that you closely estimate the number of miles that you will be driving, otherwise, the extra mileage charge could be expensive. The second option is to purchase the vehicle at the pre-determined residual value by either paying cash or financing it. The third option would be to trade it in and purchase another vehicle. If the value of the car is more than the residual value, you can use this equity as a down payment. The last option is to sell the vehicle yourself, pay off the residual value, and pocket the cash. If you lease a car, make sure it is one that will have a good resale value; otherwise, your lease payments will be higher. When you lease a car you can negotiate on the original price of the car. The residual value, however, is based on books that the leasing companies prepare. These books project what the value of the car will be at the end of the lease with a certain mileage and normal wear and tear. The monthly lease payment is based on the negotiated cost of the car less the calculated residual value, the sales tax which is pro-rated over the lease, and a money factor, which is based on interest rates and how much the manufacturer wants to get rid of inventory. The drive-away fee consists of the first monthly payment, a bank fee of approximately $300-400 to set up the lease, licensing and title fees, and a security deposit, which is refundable at the termination of the lease. Whether you lease or purchase a vehicle, you are responsible for all maintenance on your vehicle that is not covered by the manufacturer's warranty. Also, at your expense, you must have a valid insurance policy on your vehicle. Terminating a lease early can also result in considerable buy-out fees.[60]

An honest comparison of leasing and buying will almost always show that leasing not only fails to produce savings, but also, for every 3-year period, often costs $600 to $1,000 more than buying would cost. So, is leasing good for anyone? The people who should consider leasing cars are ones who need to drive a late-model luxury car in order to project a successful image but don't want to tie up lots of cash that could be put to better use. If the vehicle is used for business, the lease payments are usually tax deductible.[61]

---

[1] *The Used Car Book*, 1996-1997 Edition, Jack Gillis' Guide to Best and Worst Used Cars, Harper Collins Publishers, New York, N.Y., 1996, 6.

[2] Blue, 116.

[3] *The Used Car Book*, 5.

[4] *Consumer Reports 1996 Buying Guide*, Consumers Union of U.S. Inc., 101 Truman Avenue, Yonkers, N.Y., 277.

[5] *Consumer Reports 1995 Buying Guide*, Consumers Union of U.S. Inc., 101 Truman Avenue, Yonkers, N.Y., 316-366.

[6] *Consumer Reports 1996 Buying Guide*, 277-316.

[7] *Edmund's Used Car Prices and Ratings*, Edmund Publications Corp, 300 N. Sepulveda, Suite 2050, El Segundo, CA, Fall 1996, 33-459.

[8] *Consumer Reports 1996 Buying Guide*, 277.

[9] *The Used Car Book*, 7.

[10] *Consumer Reports 1995 Buying Guide*, 317.

[11] *The Used Car Book*, 7.

[12] Ibid., 7, 8.

[13] Ibid., 5, 7.

[14] *Consumer Reports 1995 Buying Guide*, 317.

[15] Ibid., 317.

[16] *The Used Car Book*, 11.

[17] Ibid., 27.

[18] *Edmund's Used Car Prices and Ratings*, 11.

[19] Annechino, Daniel M., *How To Buy The Most Car for the Least Money*, Signet, Published by the Penguin Group, Penguin Books USA Inc., New York, N.Y., 1993, 68, 69.

[20] *Consumer Reports 1996 Buying Guide*, 277-278.

[21] *The Used Car Book*, 12-22.

[22] *Consumer Reports 1996 Buying Guide*, 278.

[23] *The Used Car Book*, 25, 26.

[24] *Consumer Guide Rating the 1996 Autos*, Publications International Ltd., Consumer Guide, 7373 N. Cicero Ave., Lincolnwood, IL, 1996, 12-447.

[25] Annechino, 105-110.

[26] Ibid., 112-117.

[27] *Edmund's New Cars Prices & Reviews*, Edmunds Publication Corporation, Beverly Hills, CA, 1997.

[28] *Consumer Guide Rating the 1996 Autos*, 240-447.

[29] Eskeldson, Mark, *What Car Dealers Don't Want You To Know*, Technews Publishing, Fair Oaks, CA, 1995, 36-45.

[30] Annechino, 124.

[31] Ibid., 50-52.

[32] Annechino, 45-52.

[33] Ibid., 44-59.

[34] Annechino, 26-30.

[35] .Eskeldson, 48.

[36] Annechino, 20-22.

[37] Eskeldson, 15.

[38] Ibid., 59.

[39] Ibid., 35.

[40] Ibid., 41-42.

[41] Eskeldson, 103-107.

[42] Annechino, 118-125.

[43] Ibid., 127-129.

[44] Ibid., 129-131.

[45] Ibid., 133.

[46] Ibid., 63-65.

[47] Ibid., 68-71.

[48] Ibid., 73-74.

[49] Eskeldson, 90.

[50] *The Used Car Book*, 31.

[51] Annechino, 75-77.

[52] Eskeldson, 56.

[53] Ibid., 58.

[54] Ibid., 58.

[55] Ibid., 59.

[56] Annechino, 89-92.

[57] Eskeldson, 122-123.

[58] Ibid., 135-139.

[59] Ibid., 151-156.

[60] Webster, Don, Fleet Manager, Chase Chevrolet, Stockton, CA, Personal Communication, March 24, 1999.

[61] Eskeldson, 17-30.

Chapter 11 - Renting Or Buying A Home

Should a person rent or buy a home?

Practically every real estate agent, and a large part of the public, will tell you that buying a house is a good investment choice. They say renting a house or an apartment is a waste of money because you'll have nothing to show for your rent money. What is not mentioned is that the landlord must use much of the rent money to pay such expenses as real estate taxes, insurance, maintenance and interest. The homebuyer also has to pay these expenses and has little to show for it except some tax deductions. For some, buying a home is a wise decision, but for others it could be a mistake from which it will take many years to recover.[1]

What questions should a person ask before deciding to rent or buy a home?

1. Are suitable rental accommodations available?

2. Is a long-term lease possible?

3. Are there rent controls in place, or might there be a risk of unreasonable rent increases?[2]

4. How well do you know the area you are moving to? When you first move to a new location, it is wise to rent and live in

the area for a while before you buy to learn which neighborhoods best fit your needs.

5. How long do you plan to stay in the house? If, after you have purchased a home, you need to move due to a job loss, job transfer, or a major change in the neighborhood, you will probably incur costs exceeding 7% to sell the house. Thus, if you are not going to be in a location long, renting almost always beats buying. On the other hand, if your company transfers you and covers relocation costs, this may not be a factor.

6. How much do you expect the house to increase in value over time? Sometimes, a person can buy a house with as little as 3% to 5% down payment. To purchase with this small percentage is called a "leveraged buy-out." If homes are increasing in value rapidly, a person can get a very good return on a little investment in a short period of time. On the other hand, if homes decrease in price, it is quite easy to lose your entire down payment, and even owe more on the house than the house is worth.

7. Will the house require expensive remodeling or repairs?

8. What is your tax situation? Interest on a home is currently tax-deductible in the U.S. For those in high tax brackets, this is a considerable advantage.

9. How diversified are your investments? If you have a lot already invested in mutual funds, you may wish to diversify by purchasing a home.

10. Are you confident that the rate of return you would earn on the money that would be used for a down payment would be sufficient to make renting financially more attractive than buying? If so, you might consider reading Appendix E.

Are there any advantages, other than financial, in buying a home?

Owning your own home has some emotional, social, and psychological benefits. People often like the secure feeling of owning a home. Also, homeowners usually take better care of their properties. A neighborhood full of rental properties can often deteriorate.

When is the best time of the year to purchase a home?

The best time of the year to find a bargain in purchasing a home is when few people are trying to buy. This is normally during the wintertime, especially when it is cold, rainy, or snowing. There is an economic law called the law of supply and demand. When the supply is low and the demand is great, prices go up. Such a time is the late spring or the early summer, when people are hoping to move to minimize the problems involved with children transferring schools. However, in the wintertime the demand is much less, and, thus, the prices tend to be lower. Sellers at this time are usually more motivated to sell and are anxious to receive any reasonable purchase offer. An exception to this would be in places like Florida, Hawaii, and Arizona where the demand for homes may be greatest during this time because of people wanting to escape the cold climates of the North.[3]

What can a real estate agent do for you?

Purchasing a home years ago was much less complicated than it is today. Much more paperwork is now involved. A good real estate agent can help you in many ways. Among other things, he or she can offer expertise in financing, location, marketing, and taxes. The agent can give professional guidance through the entire real estate transaction. The agent might even steer you away from a house with too many potential problems.[4]

How does one select a good real estate agent?

One suggestion is to call three real estate companies and interview some agents. Many times friends can recommend real estate agents. However, it is still a good idea to interview them personally. Let the agent tell his story. See if their emphasis is on themselves or on their customers. Find out if you feel at home with this agent and believe that this is the right agent for you. The number one complaint against real estate agents is lack of communication with their clients. Also, in spite of the fact that most states require real estate agents to update their knowledge, some agents have difficulty keeping up with current regulations. Remember that you are hiring the agent. You should select the agent before you start to seriously consider making an offer on a house. Do not do this on the same day that you make the offer. In screening possible agents you should ask them the following questions:

1. How long have you been in the business?

2. How many homes have you sold in your career?

3. How many homes have you sold in the past year? A good agent should be selling an average of more than one home per month.

4. When was the last time you personally sold or bought a home?

5. Are you a licensed broker or a licensed sales agent? A higher level of training and responsibility is required of a broker.

6. What type of training have you had, and what are your qualifications?

7. What do you specialize in?

8. Are you familiar with first-time buyers programs?[5] If so, which programs do you prefer?

What is a mortgage?

To mortgage means to borrow money with real estate as collateral. The mortgage you sign for has two parts: the principal (amount you borrowed) and the interest (finance charge). Every payment reduces the amount of principal and interest you owe on the mortgage. The process of reducing the outstanding balance through installment payments is called amortization. The early payments are mainly interest. There are many forms of mortgages, but the most common is the thirty year fixed mortgage, where the interest rate never changes and the monthly payments remain the same for the entire length of the mortgage.[6]

How can a person estimate their house payments before purchasing a home?

The following is a Table of Monthly Payments per $1,000 borrowed; assuming that you paid separately any points, loan service fees, closing costs, credit reports, appraisals, inspections, etc.:

Term of Mortgage	20 years	30 years
Interest Rate	Monthly Payment Per $1,000 borrowed	Monthly Payment Per $1,000 borrowed
6	7.16	6.00
7	7.75	6.65
8	8.36	7.34
9	9.00	8.05
10	9.65	8.78
11	10.32	9.52
12	11.01	10.29

You can use this table as follows. Let's say you need to borrow $100,000 to purchase a home. If you took out a 30-year mortgage at 8% interest, your monthly payments would be $734 per month ($100,000 x $7.34/$1000). If you took the full 30 years to pay off the loan, it would take $734/month x 360 months, or $264,240, to pay off a $100,000 loan.

In addition to loan repayment, your house payment will probably include taxes and insurance.

One can reduce the total cost to purchase a home by paying off the mortgage as rapidly as possible. You should mark extra payment checks clearly, "To be applied to principal payment only." This will result in significantly reducing the number of years you will have to pay and will save much interest.

What is pre-qualification for a mortgage?

If you are doing a feasibility study for purchasing a home, you should consider being pre-qualified for a loan. A lender will usually pre-qualify you for a mortgage at no cost. The size mortgage you qualify for will be determined by the monthly payment you can afford. Usually the lender will determine this based on your monthly income and your recurring monthly payments on existing debts. In pre-qualification, the potential lender will ask to see stubs from recent paychecks, your last years tax form, and debt information. The lender will most likely run a one-source credit report. In addition to your loan repayment, your monthly payment will include property taxes, homeowners insurance, and private mortgage insurance (PMI), if you have a low down payment. PMI usually costs less than ½% of the loan amount per year. If you purchase a condominium, you must also pay a monthly maintenance fee for common services such as the lobby, the swimming pool, lawn maintenance, and snow removal. Property taxes are used to support services such as the police and fire departments, schools, and libraries. Homeowners' insurance covers emergencies such as fire and windstorms.[7]

With this information you will be able to determine what price home you can afford. There is no need to waste your time or the time of the Realtor or seller, by looking at a house that costs considerably more than you can afford.

What are some things to consider while shopping for a real estate loan?

1. **Interest rate.**

2. **Points.** This is really a loan origination fee. One point equals one percent of the loan amount. Advertised loans must quote an annual percentage rate (APR). The annual percentage rate indicates that points must be paid. The larger the difference between the interest rate and the APR, the more points you must pay. It is the best way to determine total costs and hidden costs.

3. **Lock in period.** This is the length of time that the lender will continue to offer the loan at the quoted interest rate. In contrast to this is a floating interest rate, where you accept the market rate of interest at the day of closing.

4. **Application fee charge.** This should cover costs such as the credit report and appraisal fee.[8] If there is a non-refundable application fee, make certain that your financial situation is well within the lender's limit for approving loans.

What steps should you follow in buying a home?

1. **Get pre-approved for a mortgage.** For pre-approval, you must pay a fee of approximately $50. You should get pre-approval for a mortgage if you are serious about buying a home within the next two to three months or if there are some concerns regarding credit. The loan officer at the lending institution will call or write your employer to verify salary, employment history, and the likelihood of continued employment.[9] The lender is looking for employment stability, especially during the last two years. The lender wants to be sure that the borrower will be able to pay the mortgage payments. You will usually be asked for your last three bank statements, copies of your last two tax returns with W-2 statements attached, and your most recent paycheck statement. From the main credit bureaus they will obtain credit reports, which will show a seven-year history of

all your personal loans, including student loans, and payments for things like automobiles, credit cards, and mortgages. Lenders rate a person's credit on the number of late payments, especially those that occurred recently. You can, however, write a letter of explanation to give circumstances regarding late payments.[10] Be aware that the process of clearing up credit can take a considerable amount of time. Insist on a pre-approval letter or certificate from the actual mortgage lender, subject to the home's appraisal. A pre-approval letter will probably only be good for about three months. If you do not purchase a home within this time frame you will be required to pay another fee.

2. **Inspect many homes before making a purchase.** Until you have inspected many homes near where you want to buy, you will not be sure of features and drawbacks of the property, such as the quality of the schools, prices, and the pros and cons of the neighborhood. Attending open houses on the weekend is a good way to inspect many homes in a short period of time. Also, you will be able to meet a number of real estate agents. Obtain an information sheet on each home you inspect and write your likes and dislikes on the sheet. A good real estate agent will spend considerable time counseling with you to determine your needs and desires. This agent will then show you only the homes that seem to meet your criteria. This should save a considerable amount of time for both you and the agent.

3. **Understand whom the realty agent represents.** There are seller's agents, who represent a home seller; buyer's agents, who represents the homebuyer; and there are dual agents, representing both parties. Be sure you understand, in writing, whom the agent really represents. The only thing a dual agent cannot disclose is what the buyer is willing to pay and what the seller is willing to accept. Whereas, using a dual agent could create a conflict of interest, a good dual agent can serve as a mediator to negotiate fair terms and conditions for both the buyer and the seller.

4. **Have the agent prepare a comparative market analysis (CMA) before you make the purchase offer.** The CMA shows recent sales prices of comparable homes in the neighborhood, asking prices of other neighborhood homes currently listed for sale, and even asking prices of recently expired competitive listings. Your agent can then help you add and subtract value to arrive at a reasonable offer price on the home you want to buy. Your agent can use this CMA to show why the seller should accept your offer.

5. **Most states require the seller to disclose all material defects in writing.** At the time of listing, the agent should ask his or her seller to fill out a disclosure form listing all known defects. If this form is not available when you make your offer, make sure your offer includes a contingency clause for your receipt of such a form. If the form discloses serious defects, you can rescind your offer and get your earnest money deposit refunded.

6. **Be sure your offer is contingent on financing and a professional inspection.** Even though you are already pre-approved, the financing contingency is needed just in case the home doesn't appraise for as much as you offered. Also insist that the seller provide a recent termite and roof inspection report and clearances.[11]

What is an appraisal?

A real estate appraisal is an estimate of the probable price a willing buyer would offer and a willing seller would accept for the property, with neither being under pressure to buy or sell. The most common method of appraising a home is to use the sales prices of comparable homes nearby. This method works well for condominiums and in housing tracts for subdivisions where residences are very similar. However, many homes are unique, and their value is quite subjective. The appraiser, based on experience, training, and competency, will attempt to add and subtract value for the pros and cons of the home. Thus, appraisal is an art, and not a science. It is probably the weakest link in the whole mortgage process. If the buyer offered considerably more than what the appraisal shows, the buyer can then cancel the sale if his contract contained a finance contingency clause. The price, however, can be renegotiated if both the buyer and seller agree to do so. If the buyer paid for the appraisal, he has a right to a copy. Appraisals are required for acquiring home mortgages, refinancing, and for property tax evaluation.[12] Lenders require appraisals because the home will be used as collateral for the loan.

Why is a professional home inspection important?

The prospective homebuyer should look beyond just the appearance of a home. That means finding a qualified home inspector who knows how the many systems and components of a home work. Home inspectors who are members of the American Society of Home Inspectors have passed technical examinations and meet their continuing education requirements. Also, franchised companies usually require more training of their inspectors. You should begin screening inspectors when you begin seriously looking for a house. You can ask the potential inspector for a sample copy of a report that they have done. You want a thorough report but, at the same time, not one that concentrates on insignificant details. Since home inspections usually take from two to four hours, they need to be scheduled in advance. If you attend the inspections, you will have the opportunity to ask the inspector many questions about the home and the various systems. Write down ahead of time any questions and concerns that you might have. The report produced by the home inspector is yours to keep, and it contains useful information covering all aspects of the home. Before closing, you can either insist on having the defects that were uncovered by the inspection fixed, negotiate the selling price, or back out of the contract. You should file this report and refer to it on an annual basis to plan future home repairs and improvements.[13]

How should the price of a home be negotiated?

1. **Knowledge is power.** Before making a purchase offer, learn as much as you can about the local home sale market. Find out why the home is being sold, how long the home has been listed for sale, how soon the seller needs to sell, and anything else you want to know. On the other hand, neither you nor your agent should reveal to the seller or his agent confidential information, such as your income, maximum down payment, or the highest price you'll pay for a home.

2. **Ask if the seller has a deadline.** Time is critical to negotiations. If the seller is under time pressure, use it to your advantage. Usually either the buyer or the seller, or both, have deadlines. If the local home market is hot, the competition of other buyers might motivate you to act quickly once you decide on a specific home. But don't be rushed into a purchase.

3. **Avoid showing your emotions.** No matter how much you want to buy a specific home, avoid showing your emotions. Once the sellers discover you absolutely must buy a residence, you lose your negotiating edge. Home sellers can also become emotional and greedy and try to extract a few more dollars by counter-offering a perfectly good purchase offer. Many buyers refuse to meet the seller's counter-offer by walking away.

4. **Adopt, within reason, the "he who cares least wins" attitude.** Ask yourself, as a buyer, "What will happen if I don't buy this home?" The world probably won't end. Maybe you'll find a home you like better at a lower price. Anxious home sellers should adopt the same attitude, even if a quick home sale is very important. Once the buyer and agent discover you're desperate to sell, they'll surely use it to their advantage.

5. **Avoid a bidding war.** Make your offer based on your superior knowledge of the local home sale prices and the seller's motivations for selling. If the house is right for you

and you have made an offer too low, you might wish to raise your offer. But do not go higher than what the home is worth. Home sellers should accept or reject an offer based on their current situation and needs and the fairness and acceptability of the offer. A good real estate agent will not pressure you to buy or sell, but rather give you the facts on which to base your decision.

6. **Adopt a "win-win" attitude.** When buying a home, buyers should avoid taking unfair advantage of sellers who are facing difficult situations, such as a pending foreclosure, divorce, unemployment, or job transfer. With a win-win attitude, the buyer offers a fair price that the seller can realistically accept. Successful real estate negotiations should result in a home purchase without either party taking unfair advantage of the other. Be firm and fair. But don't be afraid to walk away. There's always another home for sale or another buyer who will purchase your home.[14]

What does closing mean?

The closing is the formal transfer of homeownership from the seller to the buyer. At closing there are several documents that you must sign, such as a promissory note, which includes the terms of the loan and the penalties if you are late on your payments, and the mortgage document, which is a public declaration that you are liable for the mortgage. Closing costs can be as much as 7% of the purchase price of your home, so make sure that you have enough money available for the down payment and closing costs. Closing costs include things like loan origination fees sometimes called points, escrow for private mortgage insurance, legal fees, property taxes, homeowner's insurance, title insurance, land surveys, recording fees, and termite inspections. In some situations, health, water, and radon inspections are also required. Perhaps you could negotiate for the seller to pay some or all the closing costs except possibly the homeowners insurance and property taxes.[15] The closing date is usually about 45 days after the sales contract is signed.[16] The buyer should insist on obtaining possession of the property at the time of the closing, and should obtain all copies of the keys. However, as a safety precaution, the buyer may decide to change all locks.

When should a person consider refinancing a home?

If you plan to stay in your house for at least three years, it is often wise to refinance when interest rates drop by more than 2%. You must consider, though, additional costs, such as loan-origination fees, pre-payment penalties, attorney's fees, closing costs, and assumability of the loan.[17] Adjustable rate mortgages (ARM's) usually have lower interest rates. This option is often worth the risk, if the ARM has a cap on the interest rate that is not much above the current fixed rate and/or if you do not plan to stay in the house for many years.[18]

---

[1]Cohen , Bruce, "Renting Your Home May Be Smarter Than Buying," The Financial Post, Toronto, Canada, July 13, 1996.

[2] Ibid.

[3] Bruss, Robert J., "How To Buy A Bargain Home During Best Time In The Year," The Record, December 12th, 1998, F3.

[4] McGavock, Betty, Real Estate Agent, Personal Interview, November 7, 1998.

[5] Isaacs, Darrell R., Notes taken during personal finance lecture at Christian Life College, Stockton CA, December 10, 1996.

[6] Ressler, Ron J., Video "First-Time Home Buyers Manual: A financial breakdown of the entire home buying process," National Real Estate Productions, Inc., 1994.

[7] Ressler.

[8] Ibid.

[9] Bethards, Sharon, National Pacific Mortgage, Stockton, CA, telephone conversation January 20, 1999.

[10] Ressler.

[11] Bruss, Robert J., "How To Buy A Bargain Home During Best Time In The Year," F3-4.

[12] Bruss, Robert J., "Ways to get a fair appraisal of your home," The Record, November 14, 1988, F 5.

[13] "Pick Professional Home Inspector Carefully," The Record, January 23, 1999, F5.

[14] Bruss, Robert J., "Six Steps In Negotiating Price of a New Home," Tribune Media Services, The Record, January 10, 1998.

[15] Ressler.

[16] Isaacs, Darrell R., Notes taken during personal meeting, March 17, 1999.

[17] Burkett, *Answers To Your Family's Financial Questions*, 138-139.

[18] Ibid., 142.

Chapter 12 – Mothers Working Outside The Home

Should women work?

Yes, everyone should work. The question is where they should work and what type of work they should do. "Keepers at home" is a phrase that Paul used in Titus 2:5 to describe a quality that young women should learn. The virtuous woman of Proverbs 31 kept her priorities in balance. She sold the fruits of her garden and the clothing that she made, but at the same time took care of her household. Both her children and her husband praised her. Certainly, whatever outside job a married woman accepts, must meet her husband's approval (Ephesians 5:22).

If the motivation for working is to maintain a certain lifestyle, the wife will probably be working until retirement. Until a couple learns to live on what the husband makes, there may never be enough.[1] In some cases, it might not be a bad idea for a wife without children to work to put her husband through school, if it will enhance the husband's future earnings and self-esteem. This idea should be thoroughly and honestly discussed and agreed upon. Otherwise, the wife might feel resentment about this added responsibility. Also, the husband might have a feeling of inadequacy in providing for his family. Another thing that should be discussed before the wife goes to work outside the home, is what will happen to their standard of living if the wife gets pregnant? Will there be hard feelings? Are there alternate plans?[2]

Is it worth a mother's time to work outside the home?

Consider the following extra costs.[3, 4]

1. **Federal, state and Social Security taxes.** These are all at the top of the couple's income tax rate.

2. **Tithe.** You should give this as a minimum. (See Chapter 3.)

3. **Transportation.** This becomes very expensive if a second car is required. In addition, you are sometimes required to pay for parking.

4. **Lunch and coffee breaks.** Even if you bring a sack lunch, you will often feel obligated to go out to lunch when someone is getting married, leaving to have a baby, or celebrating a birthday.

5. **Restaurants and carryouts.** Because working mothers sometimes come home late or are worn out, they often will want to go out to eat or have some pizza delivered.

6. **Extra clothing.** Extra shoes, purses, and other items will be needed.

7. **Forfeited savings on purchases.** You will not have time to clip coupons or purchase many items on sale.

8. **Hairdresser.** You might be more likely to use a hairdresser.

9. **Other "I-owe-it-to-myself" expenses.** Since you are trying to run both a home and a career, you may feel that you need to splurge once in a while.

10. **Child care.** Not only does this cost a lot but what kind of a dollar figure do you put down for not being able to raise your children? Who do you want to teach your children?

During the first five years of a child's life basic attitudes are developed and a mother's influence is the greatest. Day care centers may mold character in ways that are not Christian. Many mothers would later trade 100 times what they earned to be able to have had a greater influence on their child. Some of the alternatives to working outside the home include selling homemade crafts, telephone survey work, and caring for other children in their own home.[5] One must determine, however, if any permits, taxes, or licenses are required.[6]

When couples put down actual dollar figures for the above items, they often discover they can save money by having the mother stay at home. Additionally, the mother has more time to fulfill her godly responsibilities in the home toward her husband and her children.

---

[1] Burkett, *Answers To Your Family's Financial Questions*, 22, 23.

[2] Ibid., 39-40.

[3] Galloway, 48-49.

[4] MacGregor, 123-129.

[5] Burkett, *Answers To Your Family's Financial Questions*, 24-25.

[6] MacGregor, 133-139.

Chapter 13 - Investing For The Future

What is an investment?

An investment is something that is purchased with the intent to resell at a higher price. Investing is usually required in order to have sufficient resources to achieve long-term goals, such as a comfortable retirement.

What are the time periods of life regarding investing?

1. **Infancy phase** (ages 0-4). If any investing is done during infancy, it will usually be done by concerned parents or grandparents who set up accounts for such things as a college education.

2. **Education phase** (ages 5 to approximately 22). Because students rarely have incomes that exceed expenses, most students will not have funds to invest other than that provided by parents or grandparents.

3. **Accumulation phase** (approximately 22 to 60). It is during this time period of life that most investing occurs.[1] This person has finished his education and has obtained employment. It is important to start investing early. Chapter 5 shows how a person who invested $1,000/year at 12.5% would accumulate $1,000,000 in 40 years having invested

only $40,000, while another person who started 20 years later would have to invest $10,000/year at 12.5% to accumulate the same amount in 20 years. This person, starting later, needs to invest $200,000, which is five times more, in order to accumulate the same amount.

Here is another example that shows how important it is to begin saving for your retirement early in your career. Three people, all age 25, think about putting money into their retirement plan. Tom starts now and invests $2,000 in the plan at the beginning of each year. He continues doing this for the next ten years and then stops contributing, but he leaves his money in the account until he retires at age 65. Judy decides she can't start investing now and waits for 10 years. When she is 35, she begins contributing to her retirement plan. Like Tom, she also puts in $2,000 at the beginning of each year, but keeps contributing until she reaches age 65. Ron starts investing $2,000 each year but keeps putting in that amount each year until he reaches age 65. For this example, let's assume that all three accounts grow at a compounded rate of 9% a year. The following graph shows how their final retirement savings compare.

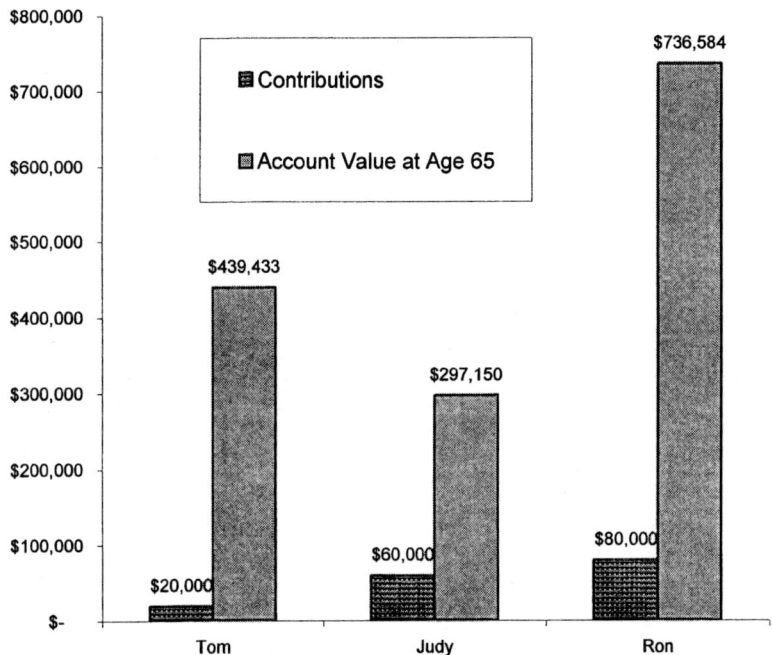

Get Time on Your Side (Based on 9% Growth Rate)

Even though Tom only contributed for ten years, his retirement plan has more money than Judy, who contributed for 30 years. This is true even though Tom contributed $20,000, compared to the $60,000 that Judy contributed.

4. **Preservation phase** (usually around 60). This is when we shift to more conservative investing, where we are attempting to preserve our assets in light of the risks while maintaining an adequate return to overcome inflation.

5. **Distribution phase** (usually between age 60 and 80). Distribution can be immediate, in case of death, or planned to take place over a long period.

How much money does a person need to retire?

You should endeavor to know what level of accumulation is needed to meet your long-term goals. When you go beyond that amount you have to ask yourself, "Why am I continuing to accumulate?"

Most people are concerned they won't have enough money when they get older. As a rule of thumb you will need 60 to 85% of your current income, adjusted for inflation, to maintain your present lifestyle when you retire.[2] By this time you will qualify for senior discounts, your car and home will probably be paid for, and clothing expenses should decrease. However, if you are planning extensive travel, your annual expenses could be more than your current income.

Another question is, "How many years will I live after I retire?" No one knows the answer to this question. To be safe a person probably ought to plan to live 25 years after retirement. If they die earlier, they can leave the excess to relatives or charity.

What sources are there for retirement income?

1. **Social Security**. Currently, you can start collecting full benefits at age 65, or you can start collecting reduced benefits at age 62. New Social Security laws will change these ages. The amount you receive will depend on several factors, such as how much and how long you put money into Social Security. To get an estimate of what your benefits will be, call your local Social Security office or 1-800-772-1213 and ask for a "Request for Statement of Earnings" card, Form SSA-7004.[3] For most people, Social Security income will not be adequate to maintain their current lifestyle during retirement. As an example, let's say your current lifestyle requires an annual income of $40,000/year. Now let's assume that you will need 75% of this when you retire, which would be $30,000 per year. For the sake of this example, let's say that your Social Security income is estimated to be $10,000/year. That would mean that you still need another $20,000 per year besides Social Security.

2. **Company Pensions.** If you have a sizeable pension coming to you, count yourself lucky. Let's assume, for planning purposes, you have no company pension.

3. **Personal Savings and Investments**. To achieve the $20,000/year needed (above Social Security and company pensions) you must have personal savings, which will probably be in the form of IRA's, 401(k) plans, or personal investments, which we will discuss later.

   How much money must be accumulated in order to have $20,000/year, adjusted for inflation, for 25 years? This will depend on the inflation rate and the rate of return on your investment.

   The following Portfolio Longevity Pyramid can be used to determine how long your assets will last.[4]

Years Money Will Last

Rate of Withdrawal (Percent of Initial Assets)

	4	5	6	7	8	9	10	11	12	13	14	15
4	28	35	46									
5	22	25	30	41								
6	16	20	23	28	36							
7	15	16	18	21	25	33						
8	13	14	15	17	20	23	30					
9	11	12	13	14	16	18	22	28				
10	10	11	12	13	14	15	17	20	26			
11	10	11	11	12	12	13	14	16	19	25		
12	9	10	10	11	11	11	12	14	16	18	23	
13	8	8	9	9	9	10	11	12	13	15	17	22
14	7	8	8	8	9	9	10	11	11	13	14	17
15	7	8	8	8	8	8	9	9	10	11	12	14

Rate of Investment Return (Percentage)

This chart can also be used to determine how much accumulation is needed. In our example, we have estimated that you will live for 25 years. From the table you can see the number 25 three different times. If your rate of investment return (percentage) is 5%, your rate of withdrawal (percent of initial assets) can only be 5%. To get the amount that must be accumulated, divide the $20,000/year by the decimal equivalent of the percent withdrawn each year. Thus, you would need to have approximately $400,000 (20,000/.05) accumulated in order to withdraw $20,000/year, if your rate of return was just 5%. On the other hand, you will see from the pyramid that you can withdraw 7% per year if your rate of investment return is 8%. Thus, with an 8% investment return you would need about $286,000 (20,000/.07). Or you can withdraw 11% per year if your rate of investment return is 13%. Thus, with a 13% investment return, you would only need to accumulate about $182,000 (20,000/.11). I don't think, however, that a person would be wise to assume that he can get a 13% rate of return on investment. People in retirement should not hold such high-risk investments if their retirement income depends on income from these investments. You can interpolate other rates of return from the chart. The chart shows that the higher the rate of investment return (percentage), the longer your money will last. It also shows, for a fixed number of years the money will need to last, a higher percentage of assets can be withdrawn each year if you have a higher rate of investment return.

To accumulate for retirement, or any other goal, you must save. To save, you must earn more than you spend. Before and during your saving you must provide for the basic needs of your family. Paul said that anyone who does not provide for his own is worse than an infidel (I Timothy 5:8). Besides retirement, there are other things you must save for, such as the purchase of automobiles and furniture, college education for children, and a down payment on a home. Also, it is a good idea to have about two to six months of living expenses saved in case of an emergency, such as the loss of a job.

Before you can save you must eliminate all credit card and consumer debt. You really have no money to save if you owe money.

Probably the easiest way to save is through payroll deductions. Also, if you receive a paycheck every two weeks, consider living each month on two paychecks. Then there will be two "extra" checks per year that you could save. When you receive a raise or a bonus, you might consider saving all or part of this rather than using all of it to increase your standard of living.

How can I accumulate $400,000 for retirement?

Very few people could save $400,000 without the "magic of compounding" described in Chapter 5. Money hidden in a mattress, buried in the back yard, or even put in a safety deposit box will not grow in value. You must invest in order for your money to grow. Consider the following graph showing how money grows with compound interest.

This graph assumes a one-time initial investment. From the

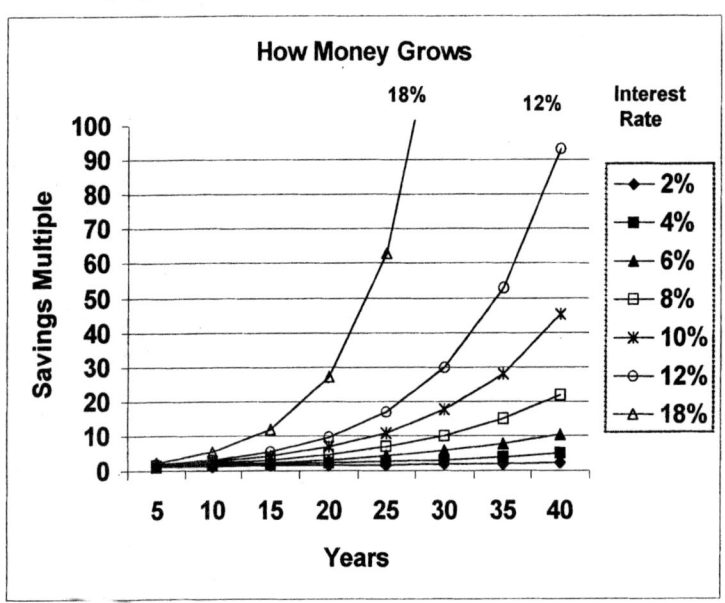

graph you can see how much faster money grows with an increase in percent return on investment. This graph was calculated by the exact formula in Appendix B, but it also can be approximated by the rule of 72 described in Chapter 5.

What are some different categories of investment choices?

1. **Money Instruments** are designed to avoid losing your principal, but many times their returns fail to keep up with inflation. The following are examples of money instruments (cash equivalents):

   A. Savings accounts in banks or savings and loan associations.

   B. Money market funds in various financial institutions.

   C. Certificates of deposit (CD's) are evidence of money deposited in a financial institution for a set period of time at a specified interest rate. Your risk of losing principal with CD's issued by federally insured institutions is very low. However, your money is tied up for a period of time, unless you pay a penalty. Common time periods for CD's are 6-months, 1-year, 2 ½-years, and 5-years. In general, the longer the term, the higher the interest rate.

   D. Treasury Bills are short-term U.S. government securities that have maturities of less than one year. These are sold at weekly auctions at a discount and are redeemed at face value. Risk is low.

2. **Bonds/Fixed** are income products designed to bring you a steady income with limited risk. However, they generate little, if any, growth of principal.

   A bond is a debt instrument (or "IOU") of a corporation or government entity that promises to pay you a specified amount of interest for a specified time period, with principal to be repaid when the bond matures. Investment risk is low to moderate for government bonds; moderate to high for corporate bonds. Most bonds pay interest semi-annually.[5]

   Market interest rates have an effect on the market value of a bond. When market interest rates rise, bond prices fall; when rates fall, bond prices rise.

3. **Equity/Stocks** represent actual shares of ownership in a
   company. Stocks have greater risks and price fluctuations
   than other investments. Stocks can be broadly classified as
   "blue chip" (typically large, well-established companies);
   "growth" (companies with the potential for strong earnings
   growth); and "small company" (measured by the total market
   value of outstanding stock.)[6]

The first widely accepted measure of the U.S. stock market
performance was the Dow Jones Industrial (Dow) average. This
was introduced on May 26, 1896. On that day, the Dow stood at
40.94. On May 28, 1996 (100 years later), the average closed at
5709.67 points. In May 1999, the Dow exceeded 11,000. There
are 30 blue chip companies currently included in the Dow.
Companies such as General Electric, General Motors, Disney,
IBM and Wal-Mart are included in the Dow.[7] General Electric is
the only company remaining in the average under the same name
it had 100 years ago.

Another index used to measure the performance of the U.S.
stock market is the S & P 500® Index. This includes common
stock of 500 publicly traded U.S. companies. Since the S & P®
contains many more companies than the Dow, it is considered to
be a more reliable measure of the performance of the U.S. stock
market. The Morgan Stanley International EAFE Index includes
stocks traded in Europe, Australia, and Far East exchanges. Total
return is calculated in U.S. dollars. This index is used to compare
the performance of Global and International equity funds.

The performance of bonds or bond funds is usually compared
to various Lehman Brothers Bond indexes. They have different
indexes for different kinds of bonds, such as Government,
Corporate, Mortgage backed, and municipal bonds.

The following graph, showing the percent rate of return of
the Wisconsin Retirement Variable Division, is an indication of
the volatility of the stock market. The variable division consists
mainly of stocks. Some years you will note that the value
decreased by more than 25%, while other years it increased more

than 30%. Their fixed division, which consists mainly of bonds, never had negative rates of return during this time period, but, of course, they never had such large positive rates of return.[8]

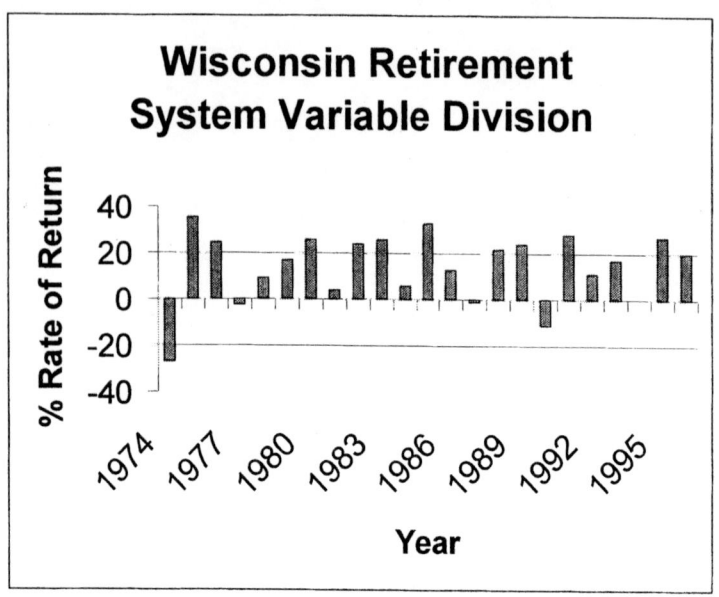

Stocks have outperformed bonds and Treasury Bills for the last seventy-one years and have kept way ahead of inflation. You will note from the next chart how a $1 investment at the end of 1925 would have grown to the following value by the end of 1996.[9]

Long-term Investment Performance

Investment type	Value at end of 1996	% Compound Annual Return	Purchasing Power Adjusted for inflation
Small company stocks	$ 4,495 99	12 6	$ 508 02
Large company stocks	$ 1,370 95	10 7	$ 154 91
Long-term Government Bonds	$ 33 73	5 1	$ 3 81
Treasury bills	$ 13 54	3 7	$ 1 53
Inflation	$ 8 85	3 1	---

4. **Mutual Funds**. For the average investor, I recommend mutual funds rather than individual stocks and bonds because of diversification. Equity Mutual funds usually own stock in hundreds of companies, while bond funds own hundreds of bonds. Both are professionally managed. Good mutual funds have research teams to select investments of good value and usually know better when to buy or sell than the individual investor. Also, an individual investor can get hooked on playing the stock game just as one betting on horse races.

There are many different kinds of mutual funds:

A. Aggressive Growth Funds seek high growth through aggressive investment strategies. These funds generally buy stocks of smaller, emerging companies that advisors feel have potential for rapid growth. The dividends are usually low, but the potential for growth is high.

B. Growth Funds seek long term growth without undue risk. The funds generally buy common stocks of companies that advisors believe have long- term growth potential.

C. Growth and Income Funds seek growth of capital and current income. The funds generally buy common stocks with potential for growth and dividend payments.

D. Balanced Funds seek to preserve initial principal, provide current income, and provide long-term growth of principal and income. The funds may buy a mix of bonds, preferred stock, and common stocks.

E. Bond Funds come in quite a variety. There are short-term, intermediate-term, and long-term corporate bond funds of both high quality and high yield (junk bonds). Also, there are short-term, intermediate-term, and long-term government and municipal bonds which seek current income exempt from federal income taxes.

Each type of mutual fund is designed for a different purpose.

The chart below can help you identify the types of funds that may be right for you.[10] Your investments can offer different financial rewards, depending on their risk. Generally, the higher the risk, the greater your possible reward. Many investors find domestic and international stock funds potentially suitable for longer-term investment horizons, and short-term bond funds appropriate for protecting principal.

Potential Risk/Reward

High ←——————————————————————————→ Low

		Equity or Stock			Bond		Money Market
Type of Investment		Aggressive Growth	Growth	Growth & Income	Lower Quality, Longer Maturity	Higher Quality, Shorter Maturity	
Investment Objective		Maximum Capital Gains	Long-term Capital Growth	Growth-Income	High Level Of Income	Income, Stability of Principal	Liquidity-Preservation of Capital

5. **Real Estate Investments.** Other than the home you live in, I would only recommend real estate investments for someone who is a handyman and lives close to the property being rented. Also, the person investing in real estate must be able to screen potential renters. Many renters have literally wrecked houses and apartments. Being a landlord can be a real headache and usually does not produce the return of a mutual fund. An alternative to owning and managing a rental property is participating in a Real Estate Investment Trust (REIT). This type of investment has a third party responsible for the management of the property.[11]

Why is it important to diversify your investments?

Own a house as well as mutual funds. The best way to prepare for the future and to preserve the investments that you have accumulated is to diversify. Another form of diversification is to invest in some global or international mutual funds so your investment is not dependent entirely on the U.S. economy.

What factors should be considered in designing a personal investment plan?

1. **Consider your age.** While aggressive growth funds may be appropriate for younger people, as one gets in the preservation stage, it is smart to shift his investments to more

conservative investments, such as balanced funds or fixed income investments.

2. **Consider your financial objectives.** If your goal is to provide for your children's college education, then the money must be available then. Certainly one would not purchase a 30-year Treasury bond for this purpose. If your goal is to provide a regular income, then select income mutual funds, which pay dividends at regular intervals. Aggressive growth funds usually pay little or no dividends, which is not important if your goal is growth, such as in an individual retirement account (IRA).

3. **Consider the risk that you're willing to encounter.** One should avoid investments that would cause worry. The Bible also talks about counting the cost before building (Luke 14:28).

   Avoid investments that cause excessive worry and restless nights that may wreck your health. Unless you can afford to lose it, don't speculate, no matter how bright the prospect.[12]

   Avoid high leverage situations. Usually, it is not wise to borrow to make an investment. If you don't have the money you really can't invest.

   Avoid investments that promise "too good to be true" returns (Proverbs 28:20-22).

4. **Be in unity with your spouse if you are married**. If your spouse does not understand the investment or is fearful, you should exercise caution.

5. **Consider the tax consequences.** The relatively new Roth IRA has tax advantages for some people. In this type of IRA the individual invests after-tax dollars but receives tax-deferred growth and tax-free distributions. It would be wise for you to check with a tax advisor regarding current tax laws. It is difficult for the average person to keep up with all the ramifications of current tax legislation.

If your goal is to reduce taxes you might consider tax-free municipal bonds.

Consider the following example that shows how tax-deferred contributions give you an advantage within a 401(k)-retirement plan. You will note from the following graph how much more is accumulated in a tax-deferred savings plan.

Advantages of Tax-deferral

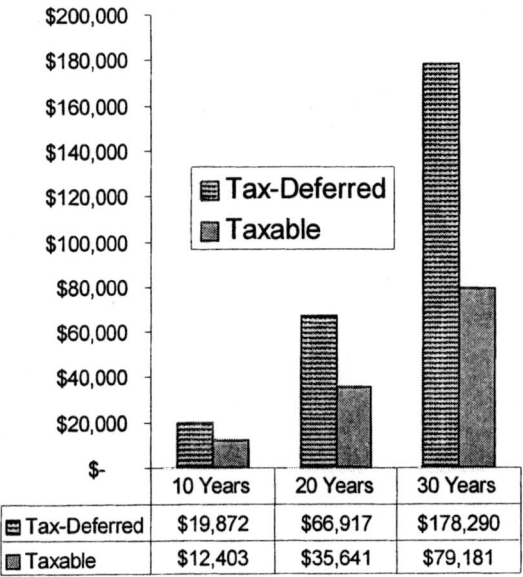

	10 Years	20 Years	30 Years
Tax-Deferred	$19,872	$66,917	$178,290
Taxable	$12,403	$35,641	$79,181

This is based on the following assumptions:

A. The employee is in the 28% tax bracket.

B. The entire $1,200 is contributed at the beginning of each year for 30 years in a qualified tax-deferred retirement plan, such as an IRA, 401(k), or 403(b).

C. $864 (amount remaining after paying 28% tax on $1,200) is invested in a taxable savings program.

D. Both the taxable savings program and the tax deferred plan return 9% annually; however, in the taxable savings plan the dividends are taxed, so the net return is 6.48%.

E. The tax-deferred plan will be subject to income tax upon distribution when you probably will be in a lower tax bracket. The amount distributed from the taxable savings program will not be taxed since it has already been taxed.

6. **Take advantage of company sponsored retirement funds.** This is especially true where the company matches part or all of your retirement contributions.

Good investing usually requires purchasing the investment and holding it for years. If you are continually buying and selling investments, the people who make the money are the real estate agents and stockbrokers.

Tithe from the dividends and interest as well as the capital gains on the final sale. "Honor the Lord with your possessions, /And with the firstfruits of all your increase" (Proverbs 3:9-10).

---

[1] Blue, 169.

[2] What You Should Know Before You Retire, American Express Financial Advisors Inc., IDS Tower 10, Minneapolis, MN, 1996, 6.

[3] Ibid., 9.

[4] Journeys, American Express Financial Advisors Inc., Stockton, CA, Summer 1996, 1.

[5] Anderson, 140.

[6] The Essential Investor, Charles Schwab & Co., San Francisco, CA, 1996, 7.

[7] Cruz, Humberto, "Here's a quick course in how to follow the Dow," The Record, November 29, 1998.

[8] Investment Earnings Distribution Reports, State of Wisconsin, Department of Employee Trust Funds, PO Box 7931, Madison, WI.

[9] "Understanding Long-Term Investment Performance," Joseph Charles & Associates, Inc., Investment Bankers, http://www.josephcharles.com/general-edu/understa.htm

[10] The Essential Investor, 21.

[11] Harden, Bill, Personal Notes, February 7, 1999.

[12] Galloway, 82.

Chapter 14 - Stewardship After Death

What are three inescapable realities?

1. We will all die. "...it is appointed unto men once to die" (Hebrews 9:27 KJV).

2. We will take nothing with us. "We brought nothing into this world and it is certain we can carry nothing out" (I Timothy 6:7). (See also Ecclesiastes 5:15.) Allegedly, when Rockefeller's accountant was asked, "How much did he leave?" the accountant replied, "Absolutely everything."

3. We will probably die at a time other than we would like.

What happens if you do not have a will or a living trust?

Unless you have a will or a living trust, the government will plan the distribution of your estate and will determine the guardians of your children.[1] Proper estate planning makes sure that the administration of your estate is handled as you would have handled it. Unfortunately, it is estimated that 50% of Americans do not have a will.

Why should people enjoy the fruit of their labor?

The shortest will that I have ever heard of was, "Being of sound mind I spent it all." I have also read bumper stickers on automobiles of retired people that say, "We are spending our children's inheritance."[2] Actually, Solomon encouraged us to enjoy the fruit of our labor while we are living (Ecclesiastes 2:24; 3:22; 5:19; 8:15). One reason that he gives this advice is that, if you don't enjoy the fruits of your labor, you may leave it to a fool (Ecclesiastes 2:18-19). However, Solomon also wrote, "A good man leaves an inheritance to his children's children" (Proverbs 13:22).

What excuses are often given for not making a will or doing estate planning?

1. **My estate is too small**. What about guardians for children, insurance, or particular personal effects? If you have children, who do you want to raise them? The state may select someone who has religious beliefs entirely different from yours.

2. **It's too expensive**. Extra legal costs and taxes will probably far exceed the cost of preparing a will or living trust. In addition, what price do you put on the extra difficulties that will be placed on family members and friends who will be left to sort out your estate?

3. **I don't have time**. You have time for the things you want to do. You need to realize how important this is.

4. **I'm not certain about what I want to do**.[3] If your concepts change, you can always revise your estate plan at a later date.

What costs are involved in settling an estate?

In order to cover costs and ease the distribution of assets among beneficiaries, much of the estate must be in the form of liquid assets. Some of the costs that must be covered are funeral expenses, probating the will, estate taxes, and fees for accountants and attorneys. By liquid assets I mean those easily convertible to cash. An example of a non-liquid asset is a closely held family business. It is very difficult to determine the value of a business if the estate involves a key employee who is a major owner. Real estate is also not a highly liquid asset. It often takes a long time to find a buyer willing to pay a reasonable price.

How often should a person review his estate plan?

It is recommended that you review your estate plan at least every other year. Circumstances change. You may have a different opinion now of the person you chose as a guardian, or perhaps the children have grown and no longer need a guardian. Your financial picture may be different and you may also have different thoughts regarding the distribution of your estate.

What are some estate planning objectives?

1. **Provide for care of immediate family.** Usually, the house will be left to the surviving spouse. If both spouses die, consideration must be made to determine the guardianship of your minor children, if any. Also, you might want to provide for the educational needs of your children. With regards to grown children, a parent should recognize differences in children. Differences due to age, temperament, demonstrated ability to handle money, spiritual commitment and maturity, marriage partners and children should all be considered. Perhaps one should entrust God's resources to offspring only if they have demonstrated the ability to handle these resources.

2. **Provide for charity.** The majority of charitable giving should be done while you are earning income. However, giving at death is an opportunity to continue having an impact for Christ. One should determine in estate planning what percentages will be given to family members and to charity.

3. **Provide testimony.** In her will, one lady wrote that her greatest desire was for her children to live for Jesus Christ.

Why should a reputable lawyer be involved in drawing up an estate plan?

I suggest you do some reading regarding wills and trusts. After becoming more knowledgeable regarding marital gift exclusions, marital deductions, wills and trusts, you should contact a reputable lawyer to draw up an estate plan that will fulfill your plan and hold up in court. Probating a will can be very time consuming and expensive if the will is not spelled out clearly and if the beneficiaries are not in agreement.

Normally, the spouse, if any, rather than non-sympathetic former business partners, or bank trust officers, will be named executor and can then hire any counsel needed. There is an obligation for each spouse to manage whatever God has entrusted.[4]

Proper estate planning attempts to minimize the amount that is paid for taxes and expenses, thus allowing the maximum distribution for family and charity. There is a big difference between tax avoidance and tax evasion. Tax avoidance is planning to pay a fair share of taxes but no more than what is rightfully owed. Taxes are needed for roads, police, parks, etc. Both Jesus and Paul taught us to pay our taxes (Luke 20:22-25; Romans 13:7). Tax evasion is not paying a fair share of taxes.[5]

One way to reduce estate taxes is to reduce the size of the estate by gifting. Property transferred to charitable organizations, either prior to death or at death, escapes all transfer taxes. Giving appreciated stock to a charitable organization is a way of avoiding capital gains tax, and you can also get a tax break. You can claim a tax deduction equal to the market value of the stock if you itemize deductions in your tax return.[6] A husband and wife together can give $20,000 per year to each of their children.[7] Legislation is currently being considered which may raise this amount. If parents transfer $10,000 worth of stock that ultimately appreciates to $100,000, they have effectively removed $100,000 that would be taxed if they wait until death to transfer that property.

Should life insurance be included in an estate plan?

One way to provide for your family in the case of death is through life insurance. As a "rule-of-thumb," families with young children should have life insurance equivalent to at least ten times the annual family income, plus enough to retire any debt. This amount can be reduced over time as investment assets accumulate and as the children age and begin supporting themselves.

Term insurance is recommended if the need is temporary. Term insurance has no cash value but provides the maximum coverage for the least amount of money. This insurance can be reduced when the need is reduced, such as when the children are grown and supporting themselves.

Whole life (ordinary life) insurance policies have face value (amount at death) and a cash value (surrender value). These policies cost more than term insurance, and often the extra money involved could be invested at a better rate of return.[8, 9]

What are the various ways to obtain life insurance?

Personal life insurance is that which you purchase.

Companies often provide life insurance to employees as part of their benefit packages.

Mortgage insurance pays off the mortgage on the house if one spouse dies.

Retirement plans sometimes provide insurance.[10]

---

[1] Blue, 183-185.

[2] Ibid., 183.

[3] Ibid., 195, 196.

[4] Ibid., 197-200.

[5] Ibid., 149-151.

[6] Cruz, Humberto, "Bestow the Gift That Gives Back: Donate Stocks to Charity," The Record, December 20, 1998.

[7] Ibid., 199-200.

[8] Anderson, 114-119.

[9] Blue, 190.

[10] Ibid., 95.

Appendix A - Steps In Balancing A Checking Account

1. Arrange checks in numerical order (if provided with the bank statement).

2. Find your ending balance on the bank statement and write this on the back of the statement under checkbook reconciliation. It is best to do reconciliations in pencil so that errors can be corrected easily.

3. Select a place in your checkbook register to do the reconciliation. Draw a horizontal line on your checkbook register at this place. (It must be at least after the last check cleared, generally the date of the bank statement. Be sure also to indicate all deposits cleared.)

4. Check deposit slips with the deposits shown on the bank statement. Make sure these match with deposits in the checkbook register.

5. Add interest received, if any, as a deposit to the checkbook register. Note as "checking interest."

6. Subtract service charges, such as for check printing and checks marked "insufficient funds."

7. Write deposits not yet credited in the blanks on the back of the bank statement. Add recent deposits not credited to this statement on the reconciliation form.

8. Put checks outstanding (those above the line) in appropriate boxes on the reconciliation form. Be sure and check the previous statement to see if the old checks have cleared. Also verify the amounts.

9. Merge recently returned checks with old checks if your bank returns the checks. Cancelled checks should be saved for three years.

10. Write amounts in checkbook of any checks that were not completely registered.

11. Use an adding machine to determine the balance after the last check you are reconciling, putting totals in pencil at the bottoms of each register page.

12. Add up the checks outstanding and move to the reconciliation portion.

13. Complete the reconciliation form by adding to the statement balance (line 2) the recent deposits not on the statement (line 7) and subtracting the checks outstanding (line 12).

14. Compare this with total of line 11. Hopefully, your checkbook and the reconciliation form will match.

15. If it doesn't match try one or more of the following.

    A. Determine if the checks, statement, and register amounts coincide.

    B. Recalculate the totals on the adding machine.

16. After finding the errors redo step #14.

17. Write on the statement "Balanced" and give the date you reconciled.

18. Write in the check register on the line you've drawn (line 3) "Balanced" and give the date.

Appendix B – Mathematical Formulas To Determine How Money Grows

The exact amount that will be accumulated with a one-time investment can be determined by the following formula:

$A = Pr^n$

Where A = Amount

P = principal (amount invested)

r = annual rate of interest expressed as a decimal plus 1

n = number of years[1]

The amount can be exactly determined with a TI - SLR + calculator as follows:

1. Enter r (e.g. for a 4% interest rate). $r = .04 + 1 = 1.04$)

2. Press y^x

3. Enter n

4. Press X (multiplication)

5. Enter P

6. Press = (equal sign) and the amount accumulated will show on the display. Thus, if one invests $10,000 at 4% interest for 36 years, the value at the end would be $A = 10,000 \times (1.04)^{36}$ or $41,039.

The formula for calculating the amount accumulated by investing the same amount each year is more complicated. If the regular amount (a) is invested at the end of each year, then the accumulation at the end of n years is as follows:

$A = a + ar + ar^2 + ... ar^{n-2} + ar^{n-1}$ or $A = a(r^n - 1)/(r - 1)$

For example, if one deposits \$1,000/year at end of each year for 40 years at 12.5% interest rate, this is the result:

$$A = 1000 \, (1.125^{40} - 1)/(1.125 - 1)$$

$$A = \$881,592$$

On the other hand, if a regular amount (a) is invested at the beginning of each year then the accumulation at the end of n years is as follows: [2]

$$A = ar + ar^2 + \ldots\ldots ar^n$$

$$A = a(r^{n+1} - r)/(r - 1)$$

If \$1,000 is invested at the beginning of each year for 40 years at 12.5% interest rate, this is the result:

$$A = 1000 \, (1.125^{41} - 1.125)/(1.125 - 1) = \$991.791$$

Thus, one earns over \$110,000 more during the 40 years by investing \$1,000 at the beginning of each year rather than at the end, if the interest rate is 12.5% per year.

Another example where $1,000 per year is invested at 10% interest:

$1,000 invested at end of each year		$1,000 invested at beginning of each year	
Year	Value at end of year	Year	Value at end of year
1	$1,000.00	1	$1,100.00
2	1,100.00	2	1,210.00
3	1,210.00	3	1,331.00
4	1,331.00	4	1,464.10
5	1,464.10	5	1,610.50
6	1,610.50	6	1,771.56
7	1,771.56	7	1,948.72
8	1,948.72	8	2,143.59
9	2,143.59	9	2,357.95
10	2,357.95	10	2,593.74
Total	$15,937.43		$17,531.17

Thus, one earns over $1,500 more in ten years by investing at the beginning of each year rather than at the end.

---

[1] Middlemiss, Ross R., *College Algebra*, First Edition, Second Impression, McGraw-Hill Book Company, Inc., New York, 1952, 181-183.
[2] Ibid., 158-159.

Appendix C - Money And Children

The following are some questions and answers that Larry Burkett[1] gives regarding this subject.

1. **How soon should a child start to learn about money?** The younger the better. Some chores, such as cleaning their room, they must do without pay, and some jobs, such as washing the car and mowing the lawn, can be done for pay. Don't overpay or underpay.

2. **Should a child have an allowance?** Occasional gifts are better than an allowance. Children should be taught to work and earn money.

3. **How soon should children start to tithe?** As soon as he or she has income from which to tithe.

4. **At what age should children open savings accounts?** At the earliest possible age. Saving money is short-term sacrifice to achieve a long-term goal. As children get older they should save for clothing and for college. The wise man saves for the future, but the foolish man spends whatever he gets (Proverbs 21:20 The Living Bible).

5. **How can I teach my teenager about credit cards?** Let them use credit cards while they are still at home. Establish firm rules and enforce them.

    A. Use only for budgeted items.

    B. Pay off charges every month.

    C. First time they don't comply with A and B, destroy the cards.

6. **Should children be required to work while attending college?** It is not a bad idea, providing it doesn't take too much time away from studying, and that they realize that their number one objective is to obtain an education and not to earn money.

7. **Can we teach grown children to manage money?** It is never too late to teach people to manage money. Often, it's easier to teach those who have made mistakes. Your financial help, though, should be contingent on them establishing a workable budget.

8. **Should I keep giving money to a lazy son?** Tell him you realize that more money won't help him change his ways and that you will help when he disciplines his ways.

9. **Should I make my unemployed son move out?** According to James Dobson in "Love Must Be Tough," allowing a child to be slothful is not helping him.

10. **Should teens contribute to family finances?** Not while attending school, except in extreme emergencies.

11. **How can we teach our children if we have been bad examples?** Make it work in your life first and then help them, but don't try to change overnight.

12. **Should I cosign loans for my children?** Parents are responsible for debts of minors. However, it is usually not a good idea to cosign for a loan. Cosigning is required because the lender questions the ability of the borrower to repay. By cosigning, you are allowing a person to do something he can't afford.

13. **How do I teach a rebellious son about money?** Children who get everything they ask for often become foolish, impulsive adults. Define boundaries clearly.

14. **Should we buy our married daughter a house if we can afford to?** This can be a great blessing, but make sure you don't usurp her husband's authority.

15. **Should I interfere if my children aren't financially wise with their own children?** If your children are truly needy, you can help. However, if income is adequate and it's being mismanaged, you may have to be willing to let them suffer a little until they have the motivation to change.

16. **Should I bring my children into my business?** Larry Burkett recommends that children work outside of your business before bringing them in to a family business. They will gain experience from people who treat them objectively. They must be willing to work in positions they can handle. They shouldn't automatically expect to take over the operation because they might not have the experience or talents. You may need to promote someone over them; however, they must have the opportunity to voice their opinion.

---

[1] Burkett, *Answers To Your Family's Financial Questions*, 73.

Appendix D – A Sample Budget Form

Budget for Month of _____

	Contributions	Mortgage,	Home Insurance Utilities, Oil, Electric, Water, Sewage, Garbage	Food, Cash, Miscellaneous	Clothing	House Maintenance	Communications (Telephone, Postage, Stationery, Internet)	Transportation (Auto, Gas, Repair, Insurance)	Medical	Gifts, Books, Magazines, Newspaper
Carry-over										
Budgeted for month										
New Balance										
Amounts Spent										
Total Spent										
Balance at End of Month										

Appendix E – One Financial Investor's View on Renting versus Buying

Sean Henessey, who teaches personal finance at the University of Prince Edward Island, wrote an article stating that an informed renter, by retirement, can beat a homebuyer by more then $2 million dollars in the U.S. where taxpayers get generous tax breaks. This assumes the purchase price of the home is $140,000, paid off over 20 years, at 8% interest and the last 20 years is mortgage free. It also assumes a 3% annual increase in the $2,800 property tax and $2,000 repair and maintenance costs, and that the home value will just track inflation at 3% a year. The renter, on the other hand, pays rent at $950/month rising 3% per year. The renter's edge over the buyer is due mainly to compound growth on a large $35,000 down payment. Also, for the first 17 years the renter pays less for shelter and invests the difference too. This assumes the renter is a smart investor and averages earning 14% per year in interest on the savings, which is an excellent rate of return.

This type of analysis will startle many people because in the 1980's home prices skyrocketed and were considered a good investment. Much of this run-up was due to the demographics of the baby boom. It is predicted that the baby bust following the boom will mean much less demand for housing, at least until after 2010. In recent years, the price of housing has actually dropped in some areas.[1]

---

[1] Cohen.

References

1. "Pick Professional Home Inspector Carefully," The Record, January 23, 1999.

2. "Understanding Long-Term Investment Performance," Joseph Charles & Associates, Inc., Investment Bankers, http://www.josephcharles.com/general-edu/understa.htm

3. 66 Ways To Save Money, Save Money, Consumer Federation of America, 1424 16th Street NW, Suite 604, Washington, DC.

4. Annechino, Daniel M., *How To Buy The Most Car for the Least Money*, Signet, Published by the Penguin Group, Penguin Books USA Inc., New York, N.Y., 1993.

5. Bethards, Sharon, National Pacific Mortgage, Stockton, CA, telephone conversation January 20, 1999.

6. Blue, Ron, *Master Your Money*, Thomas Nelson, Inc., Nashville, TN, Revised and updated edition, 1991.

7. Bruss, Robert J., "Six Steps In Negotiating Price of a New Home," Tribune Media Services, The Record, January 10, 1998.

8. Bruss, Robert J., "Ways to get a fair appraisal of your home," The Record, November 14, 1988.

9. Bruss, Robert J., "How To Buy A Bargain Home During Best Time In The Year," The Record, December 12th, 1998.

10. Burkett Larry, *Your Finances in Changing Times*, World Wide, A ministry of the Billy Graham Association, 1303 Hennepin Avenue, Minneapolis, MN, 1977.

11. Burkett, Larry, *Answers To Your Family's Financial Questions*, Focus on the Family Publishing, 1987.

12. Burkett, Larry, *The Complete Financial Guide For Young Couples*, Victor Books, Chariot Victor Publishing, a division of Cook Communication, Colorado Springs, CO, 1993.

13. Campolo, Tony, *Who Switched The Price Tags?*, Word Publishing, Dallas, 1986.

14. Cohen , Bruce, "Renting Your Home May Be Smarter Than Buying," The Financial Post, Toronto, Canada, July 13, 1996.

15. *Consumer Guide Rating the 1996 Autos*, Publications International Ltd., Consumer Guide, 7373 N. Cicero Ave., Lincolnwood, IL, 1996.

16. *Consumer Reports 1995 Buying Guide*, Consumers Union of U.S. Inc., 101 Truman Avenue, Yonkers, N.Y.

17. *Consumer Reports 1996 Buying Guide*, Consumers Union of U.S. Inc., 101 Truman Avenue, Yonkers, N.Y.

18. Cruz, Humberto, "Bestow the Gift That Gives Back: Donate Stocks to Charity," The Record, December 20, 1998.

19. Cruz, Humberto, "Here's a quick course in how to follow the Dow," The Record, November 29, 1998.

20. *Edmund's Used Car Prices and Ratings*, Edmund Publications Corp, 300 N. Sepulveda, Suite 2050, El Segundo, CA, Fall 1996.

21. Eskeldson, Mark, *What Car Dealers Don't Want You To Know*, Technews Publishing, Fair Oaks, CA, 1995.

22. Frank, Steven E., "Credit Card Delinquencies Increased to All-Time High at the End of 1996," The Wall Street Journal, March 14, 1997.

23. Galloway, Dale E., *There Is A Solution To Your Money Problems*, G/I, Regal Books, Glendale, CA.

24. Harden, Bill, Personal Notes, February 7, 1999.

25. Hayes, Laurie, "Banks' Marketing Blitz Yields Rash of Defaults," The Wall Street Journal, September 25, 1996.

26. *How to Manage Your Financial Resources: Creating a Spending Plan You Can Control*, The Institute of Certified Financial Planners, 1996.

27. Investment Earnings Distribution Reports, State of Wisconsin, Department of Employee Trust Funds, PO Box 7931, Madison, WI.

28. Isaacs, Darrell R., Notes taken during personal finance lecture at Christian Life College, Stockton CA, December 10, 1996.

29. Isaacs, Darrell R., Notes taken during personal meeting, March 17, 1999.

30. Journeys, American Express Financial Advisors Inc., Stockton, CA, Summer 1996.

31. MacGregor, Malcolm, *Your Money Matters*, Bethany Fellowship Inc., Minneapolis, MN.

32. McGavock, Betty, Real Estate Agent, Personal Interview, November 7, 1998.

33. Moffett, Martha, *How to Get Out of Debt – and Save Enough Money to Enjoy the Sweet Life*, MicroMags, 600 S.E. Coast Avenue, Lantana, FL, 1996.

34. Nelson, Sharon, "Money – A Wonderful Servant – A Terrible Master," unpublished article.

35. Rankin, Deborah, "Start Now Retire Early," Reader's Digest, Reader's Digest Association, Inc., Pleasantville, NY, February 1998.

36. Ressler, Ron J., Video "First-Time Home Buyers Manual: A financial breakdown of the entire home buying process," National Real Estate Productions, Inc., 1994.

37. Rodgers, Mary Augusta, "How I Cut My Crazy Spending," Woman's Day, September 23, 1980.

38. The Essential Investor, Charles Schwab & Co., San Francisco, CA, 1996.

39. The Record, "Study: Suicide rate higher in three major gambling cities," December 17, 1997.

40. *The Used Car Book, 1996-1997 Edition, Jack Gillis' Guide to Best and Worst Used Cars*, Harper Collins Publishers, New York, N.Y., 1996.

41. Webster, Don, Fleet Manager, Chase Chevrolet, Stockton, CA, Personal Communication, March 24, 1999.

42. What You Should Know Before You Retire, American Express Financial Advisors Inc., IDS Tower 10, Minneapolis, MN, 1996.

Index

Books written by Arlo and Jane Moehlenpah:

Teaching With Variety

Creation versus Evolution: Scientific and Religious Considerations

Master Your Money or it Will Master You

For information regarding ordering these books, please E-mail Arlo Moehlenpah at moehlenpah@aol.com

Additional information regarding books and seminars on Teacher Training, Creation versus Evolution, and Personal Finance can be found at www.DoingGood.org